AMOS
and
OBADIAH

J. Vernon McGee

THOMAS NELSON PUBLISHERS

Nashville

Published in Nashville, Tennessee, by Thomas Nelson, Inc., and distributed in Canada by Lawson Falle, Ltd., Cambridge, Ontario.

Scripture quotations are from the KING JAMES VERSION of the Bible.

Library of Congress Cataloging-in-Publication Data

McGee, J. Vernon (John Vernon), 1904–1988
   [Thru the Bible with J. Vernon McGee]
   Thru the Bible commentary series / J. Vernon McGee.
     p.   cm.
   Reprint. Originally published: Thru the Bible with J. Vernon McGee. 1975.
   Includes bibliographical references.
   ISBN 0-8407-3279-1
   1. Bible—Commentaries. I. Title.
BS491.2.M37   1991
220.7′7—dc20   90–41340
                                        CIP

Printed in the United States of America
1 2 3 4 5 6 7 — 96 95 94 93 92 91

CONTENTS

AMOS

OBADIAH

PREFACE

The radio broadcasts of the Thru the Bible Radio five-year program were transcribed, edited, and published first in single-volume paperbacks to accommodate the radio audience.

There has been a minimal amount of further editing for this publication. Therefore, these messages are not the word-for-word recording of the taped messages which went out over the air. The changes were necessary to accommodate a reading audience rather than a listening audience.

These are popular messages, prepared originally for a radio audience. They should not be considered a commentary on the entire Bible in any sense of that term. These messages are devoid of any attempt to present a theological or technical commentary on the Bible. Behind these messages is a great deal of research and study in order to interpret the Bible from a popular rather than from a scholarly (and too-often boring) viewpoint.

We have definitely and deliberately attempted "to put the cookies on the bottom shelf so that the kiddies could get them."

The fact that these messages have been translated into many languages for radio broadcasting and have been received with enthusiasm reveals the need for a simple teaching of the whole Bible for the masses of the world.

I am indebted to many people and to many sources for bringing this volume into existence. I should express my especial thanks to my secretary, Gertrude Cutler, who supervised the editorial work; to Dr. Elliott R. Cole, my associate, who handled all the detailed work with the publishers; and finally, to my wife Ruth for tenaciously encouraging me from the beginning to put my notes and messages into printed form.

Solomon wrote, ". . . of making many books there is no end; and much study is a weariness of the flesh" (Eccl. 12:12). On a sea of books that flood the marketplace, we launch this series of THRU THE BIBLE with the hope that it might draw many to the one Book, *The Bible*.

J. Vernon McGee

AMOS

The Book of
AMOS

INTRODUCTION

Amos' prophetic ministry took place during the reigns of Jeroboam II, king of Israel, and Uzziah, king of Judah. He was contemporary with Jonah and Hosea who were prophets in the northern kingdom of Israel and with Isaiah and Micah who were prophets in the southern kingdom of Judah.

Amos presents God as the ruler of this world and declares that all nations are responsible to Him. The measure of a nation's responsibility is the light which a nation has. The final test for any nation (or individual) is found in Amos 3:3, "Can two walk together, except they be agreed?" In a day of prosperity, Amos pronounced punishment. The judgment of God awaited nations which were living in luxury and lolling in immorality.

Amos is, in my words, "The Country Preacher Who Came to Town." I want us to get acquainted with him personally because to get acquainted with Amos is to love him and to understand his prophecy better. We will find that he was born in Judah, the southern kingdom, but he was a prophet to the northern kingdom. His message was delivered in Beth-el at the king's chapel. It was most unusual for a man to have come from such a country, out-of-the-way place with a message of judgment against all of the surrounding nations. Amos had a global view of life and of God's program for the entire world—not only for the present but also for the future. All this makes this man a most remarkable prophet.

In Amos 1:1 we read, "The words of Amos, who was among the

herdmen of Tekoa, which he saw concerning Israel in the days of Uzziah king of Judah, and in the days of Jeroboam the son of Joash king of Israel, two years before the earthquake." Tekoa was Amos' birthplace and his hometown. Six miles south of Jerusalem there is the familiar little place of Bethlehem of which the prophet Micah said, "But thou, Beth-lehem Ephratah, though thou be little among the thousands of Judah, yet out of thee shall he come forth unto me that is to be ruler in Israel; whose goings forth have been from of old, from everlasting" (Mic. 5:2). Bethlehem has become famous, but there was another little place that was another six miles southeast of Bethlehem called Tekoa which is not so well known. In fact, Amos himself is not even mentioned anywhere else in the Old Testament. There is an Amos in Mary's genealogy given in the Gospel of Luke, but he is no relation to the prophet Amos. And the little town of Tekoa from which he came is practically an unknown place. It is the place where a prophetess came and gave David a message (see 2 Sam. 14); David was familiar with this area because it was the area to which he fled to hide from King Saul.

Tekoa is located on a hilly ridge which overlooks a frightful desert wilderness that continues down to the very edge of the Dead Sea. Wild animals howl by night, and by day the only thing you can see are spots here and there which indicate the remains of the camps of the Bedouins. There is nothing but the blackened ground left by these nomads and vagabonds of the desert who moved through that area. Dr. Adam Smith said, "The men of Tekoa looked out upon a desolate and haggard world."

Today the nation Israel has constructed a modern highway along the Dead Sea that leads to Masada. The highway comes back through Arad and up through Hebron and Bethlehem, but it never gets near Tekoa because Tekoa is over in that wilderness. I'm sure most of you have never heard of it for, even in its heyday, Tekoa was never more than a wide place in the road. It was a whistle-stop, a jumping-off place. The name *Tekoa* means "a camping ground." It was really only a country crossroads out on the frontier. Years ago I heard a man say that to reach the place where he was born, you go as far as possible by buggy and then you get off and walk two miles! Tekoa was that sort of place, and it was the birthplace of Amos—that is its only claim to greatness.

We need to turn to chapter 7 to get a little personal insight into this man and his ministry in Samaria, the northern kingdom of Israel. There we read: "Then Amaziah the priest of Beth-el sent to Jeroboam king of Israel, saying, Amos hath conspired against thee in the midst of the house of Israel: the land is not able to bear all his words. For thus Amos saith, Jeroboam shall die by the sword, and Israel shall surely be led away captive out of their own land. Also Amaziah said unto Amos, O thou seer, go, flee thee away into the land of Judah, and there eat bread, and prophesy there: But prophesy not again any more at Beth-el: for it is the king's chapel, and it is the king's court. Then answered Amos, and said to Amaziah, I was no prophet, neither was I a prophet's son; but I was an herdsman, and a gatherer of sycomore fruit: And the LORD took me as I followed the flock, and the LORD said unto me, Go, prophesy unto my people Israel" (Amos 7:10–15).

Amos tells us he was a "herdsman." An unusual word is used here which means that he was the herdsman of a peculiar breed of desert sheep. They were a scrub stock, but they grew long wool because of the cold in the wintertime. He also says that he was a "gatherer of sycomore fruit"; the literal is a "pincher of sycomores." This was a fruit like a small fig which grew on scrub trees down in the desert. These trees grew at a lower level than the sycamore that we know today.

We can see, then, that Amos had to travel to his job. He was a migrant worker, if you please. His sheep and his sycamores pushed Amos far out into that desert. He was truly a farmer. He was a country rube. He was a rustic. He was a yokel and a hayseed. He was a country preacher. He was a clumsy bumpkin who was "all thumbs" among the ecumenical preachers up yonder in Beth-el.

But before you laugh at Amos, may I say this? He was one of God's greatest men, and he was a remarkable individual. Listen to what Amos says: "And the LORD took me as I followed the flock, and the LORD said unto me, Go, prophesy unto my people Israel" (Amos 7:15). God sent Amos all the way from down there in the desert and the wilderness up to Beth-el, one of the capital cities of the northern kingdom where he found city folk living. God called him to preach, God gave him a message, and God sent him to Beth-el.

Beth-el was, at first, the capital of the northern kingdom, and it was the place where Jeroboam I had erected one of his golden calves. It was the center of culture and also of cults. The people worshipped that golden calf and had turned their backs upon almighty God. Beth-el was where the sophisticated and the suave folk moved; the jet set lived there. It was a place that was blasé and brazen. It was also the intellectual center. They had a School of Prophets there. The seminaries taught liberalism. They would have taught the Graf-Wellhausen hypothesis which denies the inspiration of the Pentateuch and gone in for all the latest theories of a theologian like Rudolf Bultmann.

What was done in Beth-el was the thing to do. When filter-tipped cigarettes were introduced, Beth-el was the first place they were advertised and used, and from there they spread everywhere. It was the place where you could see the styles which would be popular the next year. Are we going to wear the wider lapel next year? Will there be two or three buttons on the suit coat? Should you leave the last button unbuttoned to be in style? Well, you would go to Beth-el to find out all that.

Then here comes to town this country preacher, this prophet of God with a message—a most unusual message, different from any other prophet. Amos' suit of clothes was not cut to the style of Beth-el and neither was his message. He did not give the type of messages they were used to hearing. In the king's chapel there was always a mild-mannered preacher, very sophisticated and well educated, but a rank unbeliever who stood in the pulpit giving comforting little words to the people. He gave them pabulum; saccharine sweetness was in his message. But now here's a different kind of man. When Amos first arrived, people stared at him. But they were very indulgent, of course (they were broadminded, you know), so they smiled at him. I think he had on high-buttoned yellow shoes which were not in style that year, and his suit probably didn't fit him and was buttoned improperly. He had on his first necktie, and it looked like it had been tied by a whirlwind. Everyone was embarrassed except Amos. Amos was not embarrassed at all. He must have created quite a stir. He had left the backwoods and had arrived on the boulevard. He had left the desert; now he entered the drawing room. He had been with the long-haired sheep out on the desert all of his life; now he was with the well-groomed "goats" up yonder in Beth-el. He had left the place of agriculture and had come to the place of culture.

I think almost everyone came to hear him at first. They said, "We don't believe he can preach." They came out of curiosity, saying, "We don't think this man has any message." They came in amusement, but they left in anger. He was a sensational preacher, for his sermons weren't cut to the style of Beth-el. However, today we do not have any record of the liberal sermons of that day, but we certainly have the sermons and the prophecy of Amos.

Amos preached the Word of God. Many people were moved, and some turned to God; but he disturbed the liberal element. Organized religion in Beth-el, the worship of Baal and of the golden calf, got together. They had the ecumenical movement going there, so they had the same program. If you don't believe anything, my friend, there is nothing to keep you apart. If I don't believe anything and you don't believe anything, we can get together. That is the ecumenical movement, and it was going great guns even in that day.

Amos was in the midst of all this organized religion which was plotting against him to silence him and to run him out of town. Some of the leading ecumenical leaders called a meeting. They wanted to remove Amos; they wanted to withdraw support from him; they told him he'd lose his pension if he didn't change his message. There were also some fundamental leaders called evangelicals in Beth-el who began to criticize him because he was drawing the crowds. They tried to undermine his ministry. But God blessed him, and Amos would not compromise but continued to preach the Word of God.

They had a mass meeting of all the religions in Beth-el—it was really the first meeting of the World Council of Churches—and the motto of this first meeting was, "Away with Amos, away with Amos." And the inevitable happened at this meeting: they appointed a committee chairman, Amaziah, to go and confront Amos. Amaziah was a priest who had gone into idolatry. (Does all of this sound modern to you? It's the same old story; we think it's modern, but this sort of thing has been happening ever since man got out of the Garden of Eden.) Amaziah was the hired hand of religion. He was polished, he was edu-

cated, he was proud, he was scholarly, he was pious, and he was a·
classic example of a pseudosaint.

Cleverly and subtly, Amaziah worked a master stroke. He went to
Jeroboam II and poisoned his mind against Amos. Amaziah got the
king to support him because he believed that the church and state,
religion and politics, should be combined. This is what happened:
"Then Amaziah the priest of Beth-el sent to Jeroboam king of Israel,
saying, Amos hath conspired against thee in the midst of the house of
Israel: the land is not able to bear all his words. For thus Amos saith,
Jeroboam shall die by the sword, and Israel shall surely be led away
captive out of their own land" (Amos 7:10–11). Let me ask you, friend,
is that what Amos said? No, he had not said that. His actual words
were that God had said, "I will rise against the house of Jeroboam with
the sword" (Amos 7:9). If you follow the record, you will find that
Amos' pronouncement was accurate. It is too bad that Jeroboam II did
not believe Amos because his grandson was later slain with the sword,
thus ending his kingly line. It was true that Amos had said something
about the sword and about Jeroboam, but he had not said that Jeroboam
personally would die by the sword. Amaziah was an ecclesiastical politician who was twisting the truth, and that is the worst kind of lying.

I think Amaziah had two other men on his committee when he
went to see Amos. There was Dr. Sounding Brass, president of the
School of Prophets—*false* prophets, by the way. Proud and pompous,
he was a politician par excellence. There was also Rev. Tinkling Cym-
bal. He was the pastor of the wealthiest and most influential church in
town. He was the yes-man to the rich. He couldn't preach, but he was a
great little mixer. It is amazing the things he could mix, by the way. He
didn't pound the pulpit because he didn't want to wake up his congregation, but he could sure slap their backs during the week. This is the
committee which waited upon Amos.

Amaziah, with biting sarcasm, with a rapier of ridicule, and with a
condescending manner, said to Amos, "O thou seer." In other words,
he's calling him, "Parson." "Also Amaziah said unto Amos, O thou
seer, go, flee thee away into the land of Judah, and there eat bread, and
prophesy there" (Amos 7:12). In effect, Amaziah said to Amos, "Who
told you that you were a preacher? Where is your degree? What school

did you go to? Who ordained you? Where did you preach before you came here? Go, flee away." In other words, he's saying to him, "Get out of town. Get lost." Then Amaziah adds, "And there eat bread." He is insinuating to Amos, "You're just in it for the money, and therefore we don't want you here."

Verse 13 is the crowning insult of all: "But prophesy not again any more at Beth-el: for it is the king's chapel, and it is the king's court" (Amos 7:13). That is the height of Amaziah's insolence and his arrogance. He uses here a satire that is not only biting but also poisonous. He says in effect, "Remember, you've been speaking in the leading church here in Beth-el, the king's chapel. You have been in the king's sanctuary, and he's dissatisfied with you. Your message disturbs him. In fact, there are a lot of people who do not like you. You don't use a very diplomatic method. You don't pat them on the back and tell them how wonderful they are. You do not patronize the rich and the affluent. And you're not very reverent. You tell funny stories every now and then. You're not dignified. You pound the pulpit, and you lack graceful gestures. You do not use a basso profundo voice as if you were thundering out of heaven. What you need is a course in homiletics. And you don't seem to have read the latest books. By the way, have you read the latest, *Baal Goes to Yale?*" And, of course, poor Amos hadn't read the latest book.

I want you to listen to the answer that this great prophet of God gave, this man who preached the righteousness of God and the judgment of God. There are those who like to call him a hell-fire prophet, but will you listen to his answer and notice how gracious it really is: "Then answered Amos, and said to Amaziah, I was no prophet, neither was I a prophet's son; but I was an herdsman, and a gatherer of sycomore fruit: And the LORD took me as I followed the flock, and the LORD said unto me, Go, prophesy unto my people Israel" (Amos 7:14–15). And then Amos continued with his message in which he has some pretty harsh words to say to this man Amaziah.

Now I ask you a fair question: Does his answer sound like that of a fanatic? Frankly, I have one criticism of Amos. He is too naive. He's rather artless; he's rather simple. Down in the desert of Tekoa, he knew his way around. He could avoid the dangers in that howling wilder-

ness which was filled with wild beasts, but in the asphalt jungle of
Beth-el he was rather helpless.

By the way, there is a jungle today in this world. You will find that
in church circles—in liberal churches and even in the fundamental
churches—it's a little dangerous. You're not really safe because there is
often someone who will want to tear you to pieces. There will be the
roar of some big lion, such as Mr. Gotrocks who is on the board of
deacons. I tell you, you had better pat him on the back, you had better
play up to him, or else he may give you real trouble. There is also the
hiss of a serpent in the asphalt jungle today. Mrs. Joe Doaks who has a
poison tongue. James, in his epistle, talked about those who have poison under their lips (see James 3:8). It is worse than a rattlesnake bite
to have some of these folk criticize you. This man Amos is very naive.
He says, "You say that I'm no preacher. I know it—I'm no preacher.
And you say I'm not a prophet. You're right, I'm no prophet. I'm not
even a prophet's son. I'm a country boy, *but God called me*." Listen to
him: "And *the* LORD took me as I followed the flock, and *the* LORD said
unto me, Go, prophesy unto my people Israel" (Amos 7:15, italics
mine). Amos says, "You want my credentials? Here they are: God
called me."

May I say to you, if you give out the Word of God today, you are
going to be challenged. I recently received a letter from a man in Salt
Lake City, Utah, which presents a very devious argument. He concludes by saying, "I am interested in knowing how you got your authority." I can answer that very easily. When I was in my teens, *God
called me*, and I knew He called me. Maybe you think that was because I had great faith. No, as a poor boy, I didn't even have enough
faith to believe that the Lord would get me through school. I'll be very
frank with you, I had no faith at all. I just had a tremendous and over-
weening desire to continue. Now since I'm toward the end of the jour-
ney, I have no doubt that I was called of God—and *that* is my authority.
Amos was naive, but he was called of God, and the Lord was leading
him all the way.

Amos was God's man giving God's message. Simply because Israel
was being religious on the surface did not guarantee that God would
not judge their sin. Because of their rejection of His law—their deceit

and robbery and violence and oppression of the poor—God said, "I hate, I despise your feast days. . . . Though ye offer me burnt offerings and your meat offerings, I will not accept them. . . . Take thou away from me the noise of thy songs. . . . But let judgment run down as waters, and righteousness as a mighty stream" (Amos 5:21–24).

It was a day of false peace. In the north was Assyria hanging like the sword of Damocles ready to fall, and in the next half century it would destroy this little kingdom. Israel was trying to ignore it, and they kept talking about peace. But Amos said, "Behold, the eyes of the Lord GOD are upon the sinful kingdom, and I will destroy it from off the face of the earth" (Amos 9:8). His message was not a popular message. He warned that it was God's intention to punish sin.

OUTLINE

I. Judgment on Surrounding Nations, Chapters 1:1—2:3
  A. Introduction, Chapter 1:1–2
  B. Judgment against Syria for Cruelty, Chapter 1:3–5
  C. Judgment against Philistia for Making Slaves, Chapter 1:6–8
  D. Judgment against Phoenicia for Breaking Treaty,
     Chapter 1:9–10
  E. Judgment against Edom for Revengeful Spirit,
     Chapter 1:11–12
  F. Judgment against Ammon for Violent Crimes,
     Chapter 1:13–15
  G. Judgment against Moab for Injustice, Chapter 2:1–3

II. Judgment on Judah and Israel, Chapters 2:4—6:14
  A. Judgment against Judah for Despising the Law,
     Chapter 2:4–5
  B. Judgment against Israel for Immorality and Blasphemy,
     Chapter 2:6–16
  C. God's Charge against the Whole House of Israel (Twelve
     Tribes), Chapter 3 *(Privilege creates responsibility; the
     higher the blessing, the greater the punishment.)*
  D. Israel Punished in the Past for Iniquity, Chapter 4
  E. Israel Will Be Punished in the Future for Iniquity, Chapter 5
  F. Israel Admonished in the Present to Depart from Iniquity,
     Chapter 6

III. Visions of Future, Chapters 7—9
  A. Visions of Grasshoppers, Chapter 7:1–3
  B. Vision of Fire, Chapter 7:4–6
  C. Vision of Plumbline, Chapter 7:7–9
  D. Historic Interlude, Chapter 7:10–17
     (Personal Experience of the Prophet)
  E. Vision of Basket of Summer Fruit, Chapter 8
  F. Vision of Worldwide Dispersion, Chapter 9:1–10
  G. Vision of Worldwide Regathering and Restoration of
     Kingdom, Chapter 9:11–15

CHAPTER 1

THEME: Judgment on surrounding nations

Amos was a fearless man with a message from God. Not only was Amos an unknown when he arrived in Beth-el of the northern kingdom of Israel, but he is still rather unknown today. In our country, Amos is a name that is associated with Andy because of the popular radio program of the past generation, "Amos and Andy." Actually, we should associate the Amos of Bible times with Hosea. They were contemporary prophets, and I am sure they knew each other. Hosea's message emphasized the love of God, but a God of love who also intends to judge. Amos spoke of the lofty justice and the inflexible righteousness of God which leads Him to judge.

It is startling to see that Amos had a world view, a global conception. He spoke first to the nations which were contiguous to and surrounding the nation Israel. He spoke to the great world powers of that day—that in itself isn't something unique. The later prophets—Isaiah, Jeremiah, Ezekiel, and Daniel—did it also. But the method of these other prophets was first to speak of God's judgment of the nation Israel and then to take up the judgment of the other nations. Amos reverses that method. He spoke first of God's judgment of the nations round about and then of Israel's judgment.

When Amos first spoke in Beth-el, saying that God was going to judge Syria, Philistia, Phoenicia, Edom, Ammon, and Moab, everybody filled the king's chapel. He really was drawing a crowd. They were very glad for him to preach on the sins of the Moabites, you see, but not on *their* sins. There are people even today who like the preacher to preach on the sins of the Moabites which were committed four thousand or more years ago, but any preacher who mentions the people's own sins is in real trouble. Amos exercised a great deal of diplomacy, it seems to me, in speaking of the other nations first. He was an eloquent man. Although he was a country preacher from out yonder in the desert, he used the language of a Shakespeare. He was, in my judgment, a great preacher.

> The words of Amos, who was among the herdmen of Te-
> koa, which he saw concerning Israel in the days of Uz-
> ziah king of Judah, and in the days of Jeroboam the son
> of Joash king of Israel, two years before the earthquake
> [Amos 1:1].

"In the days of Jeroboam the son of Joash king of Israel"—this is Jeroboam II, by the way.

"Two years before the earthquake." This earthquake is also mentioned by Zechariah nearly two hundred years later. According to the
historian Josephus, it took place during the reign of Uzziah. The important thing is that this does help us to see that Amos was contemporary with Hosea, he was one of the first of the prophets, and he was a
prophet to the northern kingdom of Israel.

> And he said, The Lord will roar from Zion, and utter his
> voice from Jerusalem; and the habitations of the shep-
> herds shall mourn, and the top of Carmel shall wither
> [Amos 1:2].

"And he said, The Lord will roar from Zion." This is very figurative
and eloquent language in many ways. You may recall that Joel also
used this expression. It suggests the roar of a lion as it pounces upon
its prey. Believe me, this is an arresting way for Amos to begin his
message! It speaks of the coming judgment of God upon the nations
which were round about.

"And the habitations of the shepherds shall mourn, and the top of
Carmel shall wither." Apparently, a drought and a famine would come
upon that land, a famine that would extend throughout the entire land.

When I was in Israel some time ago, I came over Carmel where
Haifa is located, and I noticed how beautiful it is there. There are wonderful shrubbery and lovely flowers there today. It must have been that
way in the day of Amos also, but now he says that there is coming a
drought so severe that beautiful Carmel "shall wither."

JUDGMENT AGAINST SYRIA FOR CRUELTY

We begin now a section of this prophecy which deals with the judgments of God upon the nations which were contiguous to the nation Israel, that is, those that surrounded that nation. This man Amos gives us a world view. The Word of God, even the Old Testament, shows that God is not only the God of the nation Israel, but He is also the God of the Gentiles. In the New Testament, Paul is the one who makes that abundantly clear. And God *judges* the nations. Although in this day of grace God has one great purpose, that of calling out a people to His name, that does not mean that He has taken His hands off the affairs of this world—He has not. He still moves in judgment upon the nations of the world, and this Book of Amos has a tremendous message along that line.

The first nation that is considered is Syria of which Damascus was the capital—

> **Thus saith the Lord; For three transgressions of Damascus, and for four, I will not turn away the punishment thereof; because they have threshed Gilead with threshing instruments of iron [Amos 1:3].**

"For three transgressions of Damascus, and for four." Amos is not attempting to give us a list of their transgressions. He could have said, "Not for three, not for four, or five, or six, but for many transgressions." In other words, the cup of iniquity was filled up, and nothing could now hold back the judgment of God that was coming upon Syria.

"Because they have threshed Gilead with threshing instruments of iron." This is the atrocity which Syria had committed and for which they were to be judged. Those threshing instruments were sharp and were to be used to beat out the grain. It is believed that with them they had torn and mangled the bodies of the people of Gilead. In 2 Kings 10:32–33, we read: "In those days the Lord began to cut Israel short: and Hazael smote them in all the coasts of Israel; From Jordan eastward, all the land of Gilead, the Gadites, and the Reubenites, and the

Manassites, from Aroer, which is by the river Arnon, even Gilead and
Bashan." Syria came down against these tribes first and actually destroyed them.

What does Amos mean by "Gilead"? Gilead was on the east bank of
the Jordan River. It was the land which came up as far as the Sea of
Galilee where the tribes of Reuben and Gad and the half tribe of Man-
asseh remained on the wrong side of the Jordan. Syria is located right
to the north and came down against them. Even as I am writing this,
there is constantly a dogfight going on in the air between Syria and
Israel around the Golan Heights, which would correspond to the ancient land of Gilead. In that day, Syria had come down against God's
people and simply threshed them, and He says He is going to judge
them for their cruelty and for their brutality.

> But I will send a fire into the house of Hazael, which
> shall devour the palaces of Ben-hadad.
>
> I will break also the bar of Damascus, and cut off the
> inhabitant from the plain of Aven, and him that holdeth
> the sceptre from the house of Eden: and the people of
> Syria shall go into captivity unto Kir, saith the LORD
> [Amos 1:4-5].

A fire is to come upon Hazael, the king, and upon the palaces of Ben-
hadad. If you have ever been to Damascus, you know that you do not
see there the original city or its original location. It claims to be the
oldest city in the world, but it has actually shifted around in the area to
several different locations. It has burned to the very ground a number
of times, and this is one of the occasions when that took place.

"And cut off the inhabitant from the plain of Aven." If you travel
from Beirut to Damascus, you go by a place known as Baalbek, and
Baalbek is in the plain of Aven. The ruins there are spectacular. The
Romans attempted to colonize it because it was such a lovely area. The
temple ruins there testify to that. But Baalbek has been destroyed, and
the great population is no longer in that area.

"And the people of Syria shall go into captivity unto Kir" means
that they were to be taken captive by the Assyrians. Kir was a province

in the Assyrian empire. It is good to have a knowledge of the geography of this area as it makes all of this more understandable. You must remember that when you are reading the Bible, you are not reading about the never-never land and you are not reading about some place in outer space. It deals with reality; even when the Bible talks about heaven, it is talking about that which is real.

JUDGMENT AGAINST PHILISTIA FOR MAKING SLAVES

Thus saith the LORD; For three transgressions of Gaza, and for four, I will not turn away the punishment thereof; because they carried away captive the whole captivity, to deliver them up to Edom:

But I will send a fire on the wall of Gaza, which shall devour the palaces thereof:

And I will cut off the inhabitant from Ashdod, and him that holdeth the sceptre from Ashkelon, and I will turn mine hand against Ekron: and the remnant of the Philistines shall perish, saith the Lord GOD [Amos 1:6-8].

"For three transgressions of Gaza, and for four." As we said before, this is an idiomatic expression which means that there could be listed here quite a few transgressions. The cup of iniquity had been filled up.

"Gaza" was in Philistia, or the Philistine empire.

The judgment against the Philistines was for making slaves. They took a certain number of Israelites, and they sold them into slavery to Edom and also to Phoenicia. The Phoenicians were great traders, and they in turn sold them as prisoners of war into slavery. They would send them all over the Mediterranean world. Because of this, God says that He intends to judge Philistia.

It is quite interesting that as I am writing this the territory we know as the Gaza Strip is still an unknown quantity; that is, it is an Arab area which is now under the control of Israel. Israel is having a real problem with that territory, as you know. However, "Ashdod" and

"Ashkelon" are still in Israel. Today you will find that in Ashdod there is a great refinery, and a new harbor has been constructed there. It will probably become a more important shipping place than even Haifa has become. I think it is probably better located than Haifa. Ashkelon is directly south of Ashdod. There you can still see the remains of the temple of Dagon where Samson was (see Jud. 16). All of these are very real places.

The judgment of God came upon these places exactly as God said it would. He said, "I will send a fire on the wall of Gaza, which shall devour the palaces thereof." In the historical record of the reign of Hezekiah, we read: "He [Hezekiah] smote the Philistines, even unto Gaza, and the borders thereof, from the tower of the watchmen to the fenced city" (2 Kings 18:8). The record goes on to say how Hezekiah destroyed all that particular area. Amos' prophecy, you see, was *literally* fulfilled. This example of fulfilled prophecy makes this section particularly interesting. It also puts down a pattern for the way in which God will fulfill prophecy in the future.

JUDGMENT AGAINST PHOENICIA FOR BREAKING TREATY

We come now to the judgment against Phoenicia. The judgment against them is not only for selling slaves—the Philistines sold slaves to Phoenicia, and Phoenicia in turn sold them out in the world—but the judgment is for breaking their treaty with Israel. Hiram, king of Tyre, had been a personal friend of David, and they had enjoyed many years of friendship. No king of Israel or Judah had ever made war upon Phoenicia. Now Phoenicia had broken the treaty.

> **Thus saith the LORD; For three transgressions of Tyrus, and for four, I will not turn away the punishment thereof; because they delivered up the whole captivity to Edom, and remembered not the brotherly covenant [Amos 1:9].**

"Thus saith the LORD; For three transgressions of Tyrus, and for four." He is not just giving them *ad seriatim*. He says, "I will not give one, two, three, four, five, six, seven, eight, nine, ten reasons." He could have listed probably a hundred, but he will mention the main ones.

"I will not turn away the punishment thereof; because they delivered up the whole captivity to Edom, and remembered not the brotherly covenant." In other words, they had broken a covenant that they had with Israel.

But I will send a fire on the wall of Tyrus, which shall devour the palaces thereof [Amos 1:10].

First the Assyrian came against Tyre, and he was not able to take the city. Then there has been some question whether the Chaldeans under Nebuchadnezzar took the city or not. However, it is conceded that Nebuchadnezzar forced the Tyrians (Tyre was the great city of the Phoenicians) to retire to an island that was out to sea about one-half mile. The Tyrians built their city there, and Nebuchadnezzar destroyed the old city that was on the mainland. About 250 years later, Alexander the Great came along. He saw that very prosperous, very wealthy city out on the island, and he built a causeway out to it. In doing so, he fulfilled Ezekiel's prophecy in which God said that they would absolutely scrape the ground of old Tyre and throw it into the ocean (see Ezek. 26). Alexander made a causeway out of the island; he took it and destroyed it, bringing Tyre to an end. Amos' prophecy concerning Tyre was literally fulfilled.

JUDGMENT AGAINST EDOM FOR REVENGEFUL SPIRIT

The judgment against Edom is because of their revengeful spirit. Back of revenge one ordinarily finds jealously. The Edomites were jealous of their brothers. You see, Edom came from Esau, and Israel from Jacob; Jacob and Esau were twin brothers, the sons of Isaac.

Thus saith the LORD; For three transgressions of Edom, and for four, I will not turn away the punishment thereof; because he did pursue his brother with the

sword, and did cast off all pity, and his anger did tear
perpetually, and he kept his wrath for ever:

But I will send a fire upon Teman, which shall devour
the palaces of Bozrah [Amos 1:11–12].

In the rock-hewn city of Petra, the capital of Edom, which is located in
Teman, everything was destroyed that would burn. The palaces of
Bozrah have been destroyed and have disappeared. This prophecy
against Edom has been literally fulfilled. Judgment came upon them
because of their revengeful spirit, because they were jealous of their
brother, Israel.

JUDGMENT AGAINST AMMON FOR VIOLENT CRIMES

We come now to Ammon, the nation of the Ammonites. If you will
notice, geographically, we are moving around almost in a circle. We
began with Syria, came over to Phoenicia, down to Philistia, then over
to Edom on the south, and now to Ammon.

What was the cause of God's judgment against the Ammonites?
Theirs was a violent crime—

Thus saith the LORD; For three transgressions of the children of Ammon, and for four, I will not turn away the
punishment thereof; because they have ripped up the
women with child of Gilead, that they might enlarge
their border [Amos 1:13].

The Ammonites were located over on the east bank of the Jordan, and
they joined with the Syrians in fighting against the two and one-half
tribes of Israel which were in the land of Gilead. They did it "that they
might enlarge their border."

But I will kindle a fire in the wall of Rabbah, and it shall
devour the palaces thereof, with shouting in the day of
battle, with a tempest in the day of the whirlwind:

And their king shall go into captivity, he and his princes together, saith the Lord [Amos 1:14–15].

"But I will kindle a fire in the wall of Rabbah, and it shall devour the palaces thereof." This is God's judgment against the Ammonites. Rabbah was a great city and the capital city of the Ammonites. Later on it was called Philadelphia by the Greeks. It was named after Ptolemy Philadelphus of Egypt. We know it today as Amman, the capital of the nation of Jordan. You can see ruins there of the great civilization of the past which was totally destroyed. Modern Jordan has been built upon the ruins of the nation of the Ammonites.

We can turn to 2 Kings 8 to see the sin that had prompted God's judgment against them. "And Hazael said [to Elisha], Why weepeth my lord? And he answered, Because I know the evil that thou wilt do unto the children of Israel: their strong holds wilt thou set on fire, and their young men wilt thou slay with the sword, and wilt dash their children, and rip up their women with child. And Hazael said, But what, is thy servant a dog, that he should do this great thing? And Elisha answered, The Lord hath shewed me that thou shalt be king over Syria" (2 Kings 8:12–13). In other words, Elisha said to Hazael, "You say that only a dog would do such a thing, but you are going to do it." Whether Hazael was a dog or not, he did the very thing he said only a dog would do. We read in these verses of the violent things he would do to the children of Israel. He was going to dash their children and rip up their women with child. It was a horrible, awful thing, and it was for this crime that God would judge the Ammonites.

CHAPTER 2

THEME: Judgment against Moab, Judah, and Israel

Thus said the Lord; For three transgressions of Moab, and for four, I will not turn away the punishment thereof; because he burned the bones of the king of Edom into lime [Amos 2:1].

I consider this man Amos to be a great preacher. The mold was broken after he was made—there is only one of him. He uses unusual expressions. "For three transgressions of Moab, and for four"—that is his way of saying that there were many transgressions; but, as usual, he will mention only one specifically.

JUDGMENT AGAINST MOAB FOR INJUSTICE

"I will not turn away the punishment thereof; because he burned the bones of the king of Edom into lime." The judgment against Moab is for an awful spirit of revenge. The Moabites had gained a victory in battle over their enemies, the Edomites, and had killed their king. You would think that that would be enough, but they even burned the bones of the king of Edom into lime. The Moabites carried their revengeful spirit to the nth degree, and God says here that He will judge them for that.

But I will send a fire upon Moab, and it shall devour the palaces of Kirioth: and Moab shall die with tumult, with shouting, and with the sound of the trumpet:

And I will cut off the judge from the midst thereof, and will slay all the princes thereof with him, saith the Lord [Amos 2:2-3].

"Moab shall die with tumult"—that is, they will go out with a real bang, and the nation will be ended. This proud nation was brought to extinction later on at the hands of Nebuchadnezzar, and you haven't seen a Moabite since then.

But isn't it interesting that many years before, out of this heathen country had come that gentle, lovely, and beautiful girl by the name of Ruth who became the wife of Boaz? Her story is recorded in one of the loveliest books in the Bible. Ruth is in the genealogical line which leads to Jesus Christ. And she had come from Moab, of all places. They were really a heathen, pagan people with a sad and sorry beginning and just as sad and tragic an end as a nation. But Ruth's story reveals what the grace of God *can* do in the life of a believer if the believer will let Him do it.

JUDGMENT AGAINST JUDAH FOR DESPISING THE LAW

Now Amos turns to the nation Israel in a reverse of the method which the other prophets used later on. They would always mention God's judgment of Israel and then the judgment of the other nations which surrounded them. However, Amos has taken up these other nations first before he turns to Israel against whom the judgment of God will be greater. The reason for their greater judgment is quite obvious: Privilege *always* creates responsibility. The more light that you have, the more responsible you are to God. I believe that you and I are more responsible to God than people who are denied Bibles and who are not hearing the Word of God at all. We are more responsible than they are. We often like to sit in judgment of these other nations round about us, but have you ever stopped to think of the tremendous responsibility that you and I have because of the privilege of having the Word of God? We boast of the fact that we have the Bible, but the important thing is our own personal obedience to the Word of God and whether or not we are doing anything to help get it out to others.

As Amos turns from the surrounding nations, he takes up the sins of God's people. He begins with Judah, the southern kingdom, from which he himself had come.

> Thus saith the LORD; For three transgressions of Judah,
> and for four, I will not turn away the punishment
> thereof; because they have despised the law of the LORD,
> and have not kept his commandments, and their lies
> caused them to err, after the which their fathers have
> walked [Amos 2:4].

"Thus saith the LORD; For three transgressions of Judah, and for four, I will not turn away the punishment thereof." God could enumerate many transgressions of which they were guilty, but here is the key one.

"Because they have despised the law of the LORD, and have not kept his commandments, and their lies caused them to err, after the which their fathers have walked." This is saying in a very brief way what the prophets Israel and Jeremiah and Ezekiel took quite a few pages to say; that is, that God would judge the southern kingdom. For what would He judge them? They did not keep the commandments of God; they despised God's law. Judah had the law of God and despised it. They even had the temple which was in Jerusalem. Therefore, God now judged them according to the Law.

Have you noticed that God did not judge any of these other nations on that basis whatsoever? He judged them for certain specific sins which are common to the natural man. Because these other nations did not have God's law, they were not judged according to God's law.

> But I will send a fire upon Judah, and it shall devour the
> palaces of Jerusalem [Amos 2:5].

Again and again, Amos mentions, as do the other prophets, that there is to be a judgment by fire. When Nebuchadnezzar came against the city, he absolutely burned Jerusalem to the ground. There was nothing left but the stones—of which there is an abundance in that particular area.

JUDGMENT AGAINST ISRAEL FOR IMMORALITY
AND BLASPHEMY

Remember that Amos is delivering these messages in Beth-el of the northern kingdom. He is speaking in the king's chapel. I think that every time he got up to speak, he would take as his subject one of these nations, and he would pronounce God's judgment upon it. Now he has even talked about Judah, and that's getting pretty close to home. It may be that a few people squirmed in their pews when he mentioned Judah. However, the ten northern tribes and the two southern tribes were at war with one another a great deal of the time. There were several occasions when they made alliances, but that was only because of fear and of the necessity to stand together against a common enemy. Most of the time they were enemies. Therefore, when Amos gave his message of judgment against the southern kingdom, everyone was present and "amened" him. They agreed that God should judge Jerusalem and Judah. But what about the northern kingdom? Beginning with verse 6, he will speak to the northern kingdom. Beth-el is the city where the king worshipped, and this man was speaking in the king's chapel. Amos is getting closer to home. He's going to start meddling.

The story is told of the preacher who one Sunday morning was preaching against various sins. He preached about the sin of drunkenness, and a woman sitting in the congregation loudly "amened" him. He preached against the sin of smoking, and she "amened" him for that. Then when he started preaching against the sin of chewing tobacco, she shifted her wad to the other cheek and grumbled, "Now he's quit preachin' and has gone to meddlin'!"

Amos is starting to meddle now. He is going to talk about the sin of the congregation which was before him. No longer will his message be about the sins of the "Moabites" but the sins of the northern kingdom. They, too, had God's law, and they were schooled in the commandments of God. Listen to Amos as he speaks—

Thus saith the LORD; For three transgressions of Israel, and for four, I will not turn away the punishment thereof; because they sold the righteous for silver, and the poor for a pair of shoes [Amos 2:6].

"Thus saith the LORD." May I say to you, I personally have never felt that I have any right to stand in the pulpit and speak unless I can speak on the basis of "Thus saith the LORD." What the Word of God has to say should be the basis of all pulpit ministry.

"For three transgressions of Israel, and for four, I will not turn away the punishment thereof." There are more transgressions than that, and Amos will mention more than that. He is going to deal with the Mosaic Law. He will not deal with the Ten Commandments as he did with Judah, but with the Mosaic Law which had to do with man's everyday life.

"Because they sold the righteous for silver, and the poor for a pair of shoes." The ten tribes in the north had the Mosaic Law, but they were committing the same sins as the nations that were round about them. The fact of the matter is that the very people whom God had put out of that land were guilty of the same sins that Israel was now committing.

First of all, we have here the mistreatment of the poor. You will find that Amos has a great deal to say about the poor. In Amos 4:1 we read, "Hear this word, ye kine of Bashan, that are in the mountain of Samaria, which oppress the poor, which crush the needy, which say to their masters, Bring, and let us drink." Listen again to Amos: "Forasmuch therefore as your treading is upon the poor . . ." (Amos 5:11).

In studying the prophets, I see again and again that the poor are not going to get justice, nor will they be treated fairly upon this earth until Jesus Christ reigns. The only hope of the poor is in the Lord Jesus Christ. We are told today that certain political parties will take care of the poor. Well, they've been taking care of us all right! Every time another politician wants my vote, he tells me how much he's going to help me. I vote for him and then my taxes go up, and they keep going up and up and up. I will be very frank with you, I find that most of these politicians are rich men. They are millionaires, and they don't know my problem. They do not understand the poor. I am thankful there is one, the Lord Jesus Christ, who is someday going to bring justice to the poor.

God will judge a nation for its mistreatment of the poor. He gave a number of laws regarding this, but I will mention just one: "Thou shalt not wrest judgment; thou shalt not respect persons, neither take a gift: for a gift doth blind the eyes of the wise, and pervert the words of the righteous" (Deut. 16:19). God put down this law to protect the poor. In that day a man might be absolutely innocent, but his adversary could slip a bribe under the table to the judge and thus receive a favorable verdict for himself. By the way, that practice doesn't seem to be out of style today. Other styles change, but this one has not. It is difficult for the poor to receive justice today when money seems to be the determining factor. Amos was speaking to a very pertinent problem of his day when even a pair of shoes would pervert judgment and cause the poor to suffer.

> **That pant after the dust of the earth on the head of the poor, and turn aside the way of the meek: and a man and his father will go in unto the same maid, to profane my holy name [Amos 2:7].**

"That pant after the dust of the earth on the head of the poor." This could mean several things, but I personally think it means that these selfish, greedy, rich judges even resented that the poor had enough dust left to throw upon their heads in mourning. Believe me, that is the covetousness, the modern idolatry of our day. God judges nations for that.

"And turn aside the way of the meek." Justice was being turned aside in disfavor to the meek. Why? Because the meek did not speak out. The old saying is true: "It's the squeaky wheel that gets the grease." The meek are not inheriting the earth today. It is inherited by those who are forward and are grabbing for all they can get. The poor and the meek were not receiving justice in Israel, nor are they receiving justice anywhere in the world today.

"And a man and his father will go in unto the same maid, to profane my holy name." Apparently, Amos is talking about a maid who is a prostitute. Both the father and the son went in to her. God says that adultery profanes His holy name. May I say to you, what we call "the new morality" isn't new at all. Israel was practicing the new morality, but God said He hated it. They were breaking the laws which He had put down concerning these things.

You can see that Amos is not going to be popular. He took the side of the poor, and he condemned unrighteousness. He condemned injustice. He condemned the fact that the poor were getting a bad deal, and he condemned immorality.

And they lay themselves down upon clothes laid to pledge by every altar, and they drink the wine of the condemned in the house of their god [Amos 2:8].

"And they lay themselves down upon clothes laid to pledge by every altar." God had a very lovely law concerning this: "And if the man be poor, thou shalt not sleep with his pledge: In any case thou shalt deliver him the pledge again when the sun goeth down, that he may sleep in his own raiment, and bless thee: and it shall be righteousness unto thee before the LORD thy God" (Deut. 24:12–13). A very poor man would have nothing to put up as collateral for a small loan except his outer garment, and that is what he needed to keep himself warm. God said, "You can take it as a pledge, but when the sun goes down, let him have it back in order that he might not be cold in sleeping that night." Now God points out that Israel had broken this law and was not obeying Him at this point either.

We talk about how just our own laws are today, but how sad it is that we will permit an entire family to be moved from their home when they cannot pay the rent because of poverty. My friend, the Word of God has a great deal to say in behalf of the poor.

"By every altar." God had given Israel only one altar, and that was in the temple in Jerusalem. This reveals that they had gone into idolatry and had a multitude of altars.

"And they drink the wine of the condemned in the house of their god." He condemns their drunkenness.

Yet destroyed I the Amorite before them, whose height was like the height of the cedars, and he was strong as the oaks; yet I destroyed his fruit from above, and his roots from beneath [Amos 2:9].

Notice the expressive and figurative language of this country preacher who had come up from Tekoa in the desert in Judah. Through Amos,

God says of the Amorite, "He was tall like the cedar. He was strong like the oaks, but I destroyed him. I destroyed the fruit above, and I destroyed the roots from beneath." God got rid of the Amorites. We read in Joshua 24:8, "And I brought you into the land of the Amorites, which dwelt on the other side Jordan; and they fought with you: and I gave them into your hand, that ye might possess their land; and I destroyed them from before you." We have already said that there are no Moabites around today, and I wonder when the last time was that you saw an Amorite.

God had said to Abraham way back yonder, "I cannot put you in the land right now because the Amorite is in the land, and his iniquity is not yet full. I am going to give him an opportunity to turn to Me, to turn from these gross sins that he is committing." You may want to say to me, "Dr. McGee, after all, these heathen nations didn't have the Mosaic Law, and they didn't know any better." Paul makes a very interesting statement in his Epistle to the Romans: "For as many as have sinned without law shall also perish without law: and as many as have sinned in the law shall be judged by the law; (For not the hearers of the law are just before God, but the doers of the law shall be justified. For when the Gentiles, which have not the law, do by nature the things contained in the law, these, having not the law, are a law unto themselves" (Rom. 2:12–14). Why would Gentiles who do not have the Mosaic Law refrain from murder? Why would they refrain from lying? Why would they refrain from stealing? Paul continues, "Which shew the work of the law written in their hearts, their conscience also bearing witness, and their thoughts the mean while accusing or else excusing one another;)" (Rom. 2:15). You and I have a conscience, and even if we had never heard of the Ten Commandments, our consciences would either accuse us or excuse us. We would either say, "I'm guilty," or we would be free of any sense of guilt. Man has been given a sense of that which is right and that which is wrong.

It was on that basis that God judged the Amorite—he continued in sin. God said to Abraham, "I am going to put your offspring down in Egypt for 420 years until the iniquity of the Amorite is full." I do not think that even the most rabid liberal would want to ask God to give the Amorites more than 420 years of opportunity to repent. I personally will go along with the Lord that when you give a nation 420 years to decide what to do, they have had long enough.

The fact of the matter is that the Amorites did not turn to God. When Joshua crossed over the Jordan River, he came into the land of the Amorites. Jericho was an Amorite city, and the harlot Rahab was an Amorite. She and her family were the only ones who were not destroyed. The Moabites disappeared, but Ruth the Moabitess is in the genealogy of Jesus Christ. The Amorites, too, have long since disappeared, but Rahab the harlot is also in the line that led to the Messiah.

God is saying to Israel, "I judged the Amorites for the same sins which you are now committing. I have given you My law, and you have broken it."

> **Also I brought you up from the land of Egypt, and led you forty years through the wilderness, to possess the land of the Amorite.**
>
> **And I raised up of your sons for prophets, and of your young men for Nazarites. Is it not even thus, O ye children of Israel? saith the LORD [Amos 2:10–11].**

In effect God is saying, "I wanted you to serve Me in the land. I wanted you to bring up your young men to serve Me, to be prophets, and to be Nazarites." But what had happened?—

> **But ye gave the Nazarites wine to drink; and commanded the prophets, saying, Prophesy not [Amos 2:12].**

A Nazarite was an Israelite who took a vow voluntarily to dedicate himself to God. There were three things that a Nazarite did not do. First, he did not cut his hair. Why? Because for a man to have long hair, Paul says, is a shame to him (see 1 Cor. 11:14). When I look around me today and see some fellows, I agree with Paul that it is sort of a shame for a man to have long hair. But I will simply say that the Nazarites let their hair grow because they were willing to bear shame.

The second thing was that a Nazarite was not permitted to drink wine or touch any fruit of the vine. They were not to eat grapes or even raisins. The Israelites were causing a Nazarite to break his vow when they gave him wine.

The Nazarite also was not to touch a dead body or come near to one. When a loved one died, he did not even attend the funeral. This was done as an evidence of the fact that he had put God first in his life.

"And commanded the prophets, saying, Prophesy not." The people said to the prophets, "We don't want to hear you. We don't want to have any messages from you at all." They refused to listen to God's prophets.

Let me again make an analogy to our own nation today. We are following the same pattern that Rome followed when she went down. Rome was not destroyed from the outside, and I do not believe that there will come a missile over the North Pole which will destroy America. I think the missile which will destroy us is the propaganda that is abroad today. Through it we have become convinced that we are a sophisticated, very progressive nation and that nothing can happen to us. The truth is that we are probably going down as fast as any nation in history. A leading statesman has said, "This nation has gone down faster in the past ten years than it did in its entire history from its inception." How true that is!

There are two things which are bringing us down as a nation. One of them is drunkenness. There are a shocking number of alcoholics in this country. A majority of the fatal accidents that take place on our highways involve drunk drivers. Yet we are criticized if we speak out about this. We make laws concerning the use and abuse of drugs, and I agree with those laws; but what about liquor, my friend? Liquor is one of the things that is destroying us as a nation.

The other thing that characterizes us today is that we are not hearing the Word of God. The liberal preacher is the popular preacher. If we are going to hear the opinion of a minister on television, it will be the liberal preacher. The other day there was a panel discussion on television about abortion. They included a minister on the panel. You guessed it—he was a liberal. Recently I also viewed a discussion about women's rights. Again, the minister who spoke was a liberal. They do not ask a Bible-teaching preacher to tell what God has said on the subject. And yet we talk about religious liberty! My friend, the voice of God is not being heard in this land except for a few of us weak fellows who are trying to declare the Word of God.

The same thing was happening in Israel. Amos said, "You are giving the Nazarite wine, causing him to break his vow and turning him from God. And you say to the prophets, 'Prophesy not.' You say to me, 'Don't talk like that. We want to hear something that will butter us up and make us feel good.'"

> **Behold, I am pressed under you, as a cart is pressed that is full of sheaves [Amos 2:13].**

There are different ways of interpreting this verse, even different ways of translating it. It is the belief of some that it is rather degrading to think of God as being pressed down like a cart. I do not feel that way about it. God is saying here, "You have put Me in a difficult situation. You are My people. I put you in the land, and I put the Amorite out. Now here you are committing the same sins they commit! Do you expect Me to shut My eyes to your sin because you are My people? I'm being pressed down 'as a cart is pressed that is full of sheaves.'"

> **Therefore the flight shall perish from the swift, and the strong shall not strengthen his force, neither shall the mighty deliver himself:**
>
> **Neither shall he stand that handleth the bow; and he that is swift of foot shall not deliver himself: neither shall he that rideth the horse deliver himself.**
>
> **And he that is courageous among the mighty shall flee away naked in that day, saith the LORD [Amos 2:14–16].**

There are some expositors who believe this refers to the earthquake mentioned in the first verse of Amos' prophecy. I do not think there is any reference here to an earthquake at all. The point is this: Israel was a strong nation. God had kept the enemy out, and no one had ever advanced into their land. Now everything is breaking down, even the walls of the city. The enemy has come in, and the strong are no longer strong.

We as a nation today ought to do a little thinking about what has happened in our land. In two world wars we were able to cross the sea and bring an end to the conflict. In that we became a great nation, and we were very proud. We felt we didn't need God at all—we had the atom bomb. Then a little country called North Vietnam came along, and we thought that we would subdue them overnight. I am not attempting to fix blame on anyone, but I do say that America should have learned a lesson from that. We did not win a victory. We were never able to subdue the little enemy, and we were divided at home. It is true that we did not want to bring the full force of our military power to bear, but this reveals the fact that we are becoming weak as a nation. We ought to wake up instead of shutting our eyes to the condition of our land. We ought to begin to call attention to the fact that God is already beginning to bring us down as He brought His own people down.

God said to Israel, "You are becoming weak, and you do not seem to realize that I have already begun to judge you." That was Amos' message, and it is no wonder that the people wanted to run him out of town. It is no wonder they didn't want to hear the message he had for them. And he is not through yet!

CHAPTER 3

THEME: God's charge against the whole house of Israel

Hear this word that the LORD hath spoken against you, O children of Israel, against the whole family which I brought up from the land of Egypt, saying [Amos 3:1].

Now God is ignoring the fact that the nation is split. He says that He is speaking to the whole family of Israel which He brought out of Egypt. In His eyes there were not two nations but one. The twelve tribes are one family before Him.

You only have I known of all the families of the earth: therefore I will punish you for all your iniquities [Amos 3:2].

This is getting right down to where the rubber meets the road, which shows the kind of prophet Amos was. He didn't beat around the bush. He didn't mince words. He comes right out and says that God will punish Israel for her iniquities. It's too bad the politicians and the priests wouldn't listen to him. If they had, it could have been a different story for Israel.

"You only have I known of all the families of the earth." After the disaster of the Flood, man was still in such sin that at the Tower of Babel all mankind had departed from God. It was total apostasy. Then God reached down to Ur of the Chaldees and called a man, told him to get away from his home of idolatry and to go to a place which He would show him. God said that from this one man, Abraham, He would make a nation and give him a land. This is what God means when He says, "You only have I known of all the families of the earth."

In order to get a message through to the world, God had to use this method. At the Tower of Babel, man was not building an escape in case there would be another flood—that was never the point. It was an altar that was built, apparently, to the sun. It was a place of worship. After the Flood men had the false idea that the god of darkness and the god of the storm had brought the Flood. So now they are going to worship the sun. It was sun worship that prevailed in the Tigris-Euphrates valley and continues until this very day. In the religion of Zoroaster there is the worship of light even down to the present.

God chose Abraham from among the nations, out of Abraham He brought forth the nation Israel, and to the nation He gave His Word. His purpose was that this nation would give His Word to the world. And this is God's purpose for us, my friend. For this reason I am attempting to get out His whole Word—all sixty-six books—by all means available to me.

"Therefore I will punish you for all your iniquities." God is saying, "I intend to judge you." The nation Israel occupied a unique relationship to God. God had given to them His commandments. And the reason He would judge Israel so severely is because they had broken so many of His commandments. You see, light creates responsibility. An enlightened nation has a greater responsibility than a nation which is in darkness.

This is a great principle that God puts down here. He intends to judge in a harsher manner those who have received light than those who are in darkness. The Lord Jesus also mentioned the fact that some would receive fewer stripes and others would receive more stripes. Many times I have made the statement that I would rather be a heathen Hottentot in the darkest corner of this earth, bowing down before an ugly, hideous idol of stone, than to be the so-called civilized man in this country, sitting in church on Sunday morning while he hears the Gospel preached and does nothing about it. The man who hears the Word of God has a greater responsibility than the man who doesn't. Therefore, there are different degrees of punishment.

God makes it clear that He intends to punish them for their iniquities. Now a great many people today like to hear of the love of God. The love of God is indeed wonderful, and I don't think any teacher has emphasized it more than I have. It is something we need to rest upon and rejoice in. The love of God is manifested in the cross of Christ— "For God so loved the world, that he gave his only begotten Son . . ."

(John 3:16). The cross is where God revealed His love, and when that love is rejected, there is nothing left but punishment. A great many folk feel that God should not punish; but, since they are not running the universe, I am of the opinion that their viewpoint will not be followed. God has already said that He is holy, righteous, just, and that He intends to punish. Judgment upon sin is the logical consequence.

In fact, there will be a set of questions asked and answered, which reveal what a logical matter-of-fact prophet Amos really was. He deals with certain basic truths. He was a man from the edge of the wilderness down in Tekoa, and he draws from his long experience down there. He takes his lessons from the world of nature. He learned some things that folk still need to learn today.

I shall never forget the day my daughter went to a dairy on a school excursion. She had grown up in Pasadena, so she was a city girl. She came home from the excursion that day with the most exciting news you have ever heard. She told us that milk came from a *cow!* She had thought that milk came from the market and had originated there.

Well, this man Amos is a country man, and he has observed many wonderful things in nature.

Notice his first question:

Can two walk together, except they be agreed? [Amos 3:3].

Can two walk together? Yes, but they cannot go together unless they are in agreement. I watched a young couple the other day who hadn't been married long. They were walking down the street arm in arm. All of a sudden she turned around, stamped her little foot, and started walking back toward their home—but he kept on going. They weren't walking together any more because there had been some disagreement. Can two walk together, except they be agreed?

Here is a cause and an effect. The cause: there must be agreement if you are to walk together with God. The effect: you will walk with Him when you are in agreement. This doesn't mean that God will come over and agree with you. You and I will have to go over to His side and agree with Him. As someone has said, God rides triumphantly in His own chariot. And if you don't want to get under the wheels of that chariot, you had better get aboard and ride. After all, God is carrying through *His* purpose in the world.

It was very interesting to me to visit England and see Windsor Castle and Hampton Court. I think of Henry VI, Henry VIII, and Richard II, who were some of the boys who made the Tower of London famous because they sent many there who lost their heads. They had their way for a while—especially Henry VIII, but no one today is paying much attention to what Henry VIII thought or to what he did. My friend, God is running His universe *His* way and is not asking advice from little man. If you and I are going to walk with God, we will have to go His way. Amos has stated a great principle in his first question: "Can two walk together, except they be agreed?"

Now here is Amos' second question:

Will a lion roar in the forest, when he hath no prey? will a young lion cry out of his den, if he have taken nothing? [Amos 3:4].

"Will a lion roar in the forest, when he hath no prey?" Of course not. A lion moves about stealthily, quietly, silently on his padded feet. He is noiseless until he pounces on his prey. When he has captured his prey, then you can hear him roar.

"Will a young lion cry out of his den, if he have taken nothing?" No. The little lion doesn't make a sound because his mamma told him to keep quiet while she was away getting something for him to eat. But when she comes back with his supper, then he lets out a cry—but not until then.

You see, there is always a cause and a result. And the judgment of God *will* follow man's iniquity.

Amos has another question:

Can a bird fall in a snare upon the earth, where no gin is for him? shall one take up a snare from the earth, and have taken nothing at all? [Amos 3:5].

A "gin" is a trap. Of course a bird in not going to get caught in a snare unless a trap is laid for him. When I was a boy, they used to tell me that I could catch a bird if I put salt on its tail. So I ran all over the neighborhood trying to get salt on a bird's tail—and found it didn't work! I found that I couldn't catch a bird without a trap. In nature there is always the principle of cause and effect. If you are going to catch a bird, you will have to have a trap.

Now here is another question: "Shall one take up a snare from the earth, and have taken nothing at all?" A man is not going to keep setting a trap if he doesn't catch anything in it. I used to have six traps when I was a boy. In the fall of the year, I would ride down on my bicycle every morning before school to see if I had caught anything. In one of those six traps I would usually have a possum or a rabbit, sometimes I would have a skunk (I always gave the skunk to a friend of mine. Although I could get more for the fur, I didn't care for the scent.) After I had left a trap in a place day after day and caught nothing, it would be foolish for me to continue to leave the trap there; so I would move it to some other place. If you are going to put out a trap, you expect to catch something in the trap.

> **Shall a trumpet be blown in the city, and the people not be afraid? shall there be evil in a city, and the LORD hath not done it? [Amos 3:6].**

"Shall a trumpet be blown in the city, and the people not be afraid?" God has said that He is going to judge the people, and judgment *is* coming. It is rather *foolish* to fail to respond. It should have had an effect on their lives, but they are not listening to the prophet—any more than our nation is listening to the Word of God today.

"Shall there be evil in a city, and the LORD hath not done it?" First of all, let's understand that the word *"evil"* does not mean something which is sinful or wrong. It means calamity or judgment. Amos is saying, "Shall there be a calamity in the city, and the Lord has not done it?" This means, my friend, that there is no such thing as an accident in the life of a child of God. There *must* be a cause for the effect. God is not moving this universe in a foolish, idle manner.

Therefore, when calamity strikes, there is a lesson to be learned from it. I believe that if America had learned the lesson of the "dust bowl" and of the drought period and of the depression, we would never have had to fight World War II. But we did not learn. Neither did we listen to God's warning in World War II, so we fought a tragic war in Vietnam, and still we are not listening to God. My friend, God will not let any nation dwell in peace and prosperity when it is in sin. Oh, it may have a period of peace and prosperity, but judgment *will* come.

Amos asks seven questions which illustrate that for every effect there is a cause and that the judgment of God which is coming is not accidental but is a result caused by the sin of the people.

Surely the Lord God will do nothing, but he revealeth his secret unto his servants the prophets [Amos 3:7].

Amos is saying that God will not move in judgment until He gives His message to the prophets. He will let them know what He intends to do.

The lion hath roared, who will not fear? the Lord God hath spoken, who can but prophesy? [Amos 3:8].

The prophets were giving God's message to Israel.

The problem in our day is not that people do not have a Word from God; the problem is that they will not hear that Word from God. His warnings are given in His Word. I feel that the Bible is more up to date than tomorrow morning's newspaper. After all, tomorrow morning's paper will be out of date by noon when the afternoon edition comes off the press. But the Word of God will be just as good the next day and on to the end of time.

It has always been God's method to reveal information to those who are His own concerning future judgment. You will recall that during Noah's day, God told him of a coming flood judgment and gave Noah 120 years to warn his generation. But the world did not heed his message. Also, remember that God let Abraham know ahead of time regarding the destruction of Sodom and Gomorrah. It is a good thing He did that because if He had not, it would have given Abraham a wrong viewpoint of the almighty God. It has always been God's method to reveal such things to His own. When He was here in the flesh, He told His disciples, "Henceforth I call you not servants; for the servant knoweth not what his lord doeth: but I have called you friends; for all things that I have heard of my Father I have made known unto you" (John 15:15). There are many examples of this throughout the Bible. He gave a forewarning to Joseph in Egypt of the seven years of famine that were to come upon the earth. Also, Elijah was forewarned of the drought that would come upon Israel. He walked into the courts of Ahab and Jezebel to announce to them that they were in for a drought—". . . As the LORD God of Israel liveth, before whom I stand, there shall not be dew nor rain these years, but according to my word—[and I'm not saying anything!]" (1 Kings 17:1). Then he walked out of the court and dropped out of sight for over three years. Since it is God's method to warn of impending judgment, our Lord told His apostles when He was gathered with them on the Mount of Olives that Jerusalem would be destroyed—not one stone would be left upon another.

It is God's method always to give a warning of impending judgment, and that is all that Amos is doing here although his contemporaries are very critical of him. Folk just don't want to hear about judgment. They would much rather hide their head in the sand like the proverbial ostrich. Some people will not even go to a doctor because they do not want to know that something is wrong with them. The human family does not want to hear the bad news of judgment which is coming. If you preach and teach the truth, they will say you are a pessimist, a killjoy, a gloom-caster. However, God follows the principle that for every effect there is a cause, and God sends judgment only upon a sinning people.

God also makes it clear that the prophet is *obligated* to give His message—regardless of what it is. In fact, he ought to be in fear if he fails to relay God's message to the people. Frankly, I feel sorry today for the liberal who is refusing to declare God's message. He ought to be in fear. "The lion hath roared, who will not fear?" God has spoken. Now let's speak what God has to say. Let's get off this social gospel—which is almost like being on dope and taking a trip of sweetness and light, rose water and sunshine, expecting everything to work out beautifully. Well, I have been told all my life by politicians and preachers that there is a pot of gold at the end of the rainbow and we are going to arrive there shortly. But I've been on this trip for most of this century, and we haven't arrived yet—in fact, conditions get worse and worse. They refuse to face up to the fact that the real problem is sin in the heart of man.

Publish in the palaces at Ashdod, and in the palaces in the land of Egypt, and say, Assemble yourselves upon the mountains of Samaria, and behold the great tumults in the midst thereof, and the oppressed in the midst thereof [Amos 3:9].

"Publish in the palaces at Ashdod." Ashdod is in the country of the Philistines. At the time I am writing this, Israel has Ashdod. They have built a great many apartment buildings, a man-made harbor, and have erected a big oil refinery there so that oil is brought into Ashdod today.

A friend of mine who teaches prophecy attempts to find fulfilled prophecy in modern Palestine. When the oil pipeline came into Haifa in the northern part of Israel and an oil refinery was in operation and oil tankers were loading there, my friend said, "See, here is the fulfillment of the prophecy that Asher will dip his foot in oil!" However, that pipeline was cut, and the only oil brought into Haifa was by tankers. Now there is a pipeline across the Negeb from the Red Sea to Ashdod. Oil is piped from the tankers across to the refinery in Ashdod. It looks like it would be the tribe of Dan that gets its foot in oil today! My friend doesn't mention the fulfillment of this particular prophecy anymore because he can see it doesn't apply. I personally do not think that prophecy is being fulfilled in that land at all. However, I *do* see the setting of the stage that will later on bring the fulfillment of prophecy. It is foolish to pick out these little specific prophecies and insist that they are currently being fulfilled.

However, when Amos was giving his prophecy, Ashdod was a prominent city of the Philistines and stands here in this particular verse as representative for all of Philistia. "And in the palaces in the land of Egypt." God was instructing His prophets to spread this word upon the palaces of Ashdod and Egypt. Now notice what the invitation was—

"Assemble yourselves upon the mountains of Samaria, and behold the great tumults in the midst thereof, and the oppressed in the midst thereof." Samaria was the capital of the northern kingdom of Israel, and the palace of Ahab and Jezebel was there. Samaria was built on one mountain, but there were other mountains surrounding the city. From these surrounding mountains, people could see what was going on in the city. Sin was going great guns. "The great tumults" were riots caused by the oppression of the poor. If the pagan nations of Philistia and Egypt condemned Israel, wouldn't a holy God condemn them?

> **For they know not to do right, saith the Lord, who store up violence and robbery in their palaces [Amos 3:10].**

Samaria was storing up in their palaces that which they had been stealing.

> **Therefore thus saith the Lord God; An adversary there shall be even round about the land; and he shall bring down thy strength from thee, and thy palaces shall be spoiled [Amos 3:11].**

My friend, today the palaces of Samaria lie in ruins—I have seen them on several occasions.

> **Thus saith the Lord; As the shepherd taketh out of the mouth of the lion two legs, or a piece of an ear; so shall the children of Israel be taken out that dwell in Samaria in the corner of a bed, and in Damascus in a couch [Amos 3:12].**

After God's judgment has fallen on Samaria, the remaining remnant is likened to a piece of an ear and two legs which are all that are left of a lamb after a lion has devoured it. You see, God's judgment was severe because Samaria had light from heaven which made their responsibility great.

> **Hear ye, and testify in the house of Jacob, saith the Lord GOD, the God of hosts,**
>
> **That in the day that I shall visit the transgressions of Israel upon him I will also visit the altars of Beth-el: and the horns of the altar shall be cut off, and fall to the ground [Amos 3:13–14].**

"The altars of Beth-el" refer to the worship of the golden calf. "The horns of the altar shall be cut off." God is saying that He intends to remove this gross idolatry from His land.

> **And I will smite the winter house with the summer house; and the houses of ivory shall perish, and the great houses shall have an end, saith the LORD [Amos 3:15].**

"The houses of ivory shall perish." Ahab and Jezebel had built on the top of the hill in Samaria. Their tremendous palace was in a most beautiful location. I particularly noticed that on my last trip there. That palace covers the very brow of the hill, the tip-top of the hill. From their palace they could look in every direction. To the west they could see the Mediterranean Sea on a clear day. To the east they could see the Jordan valley. To the north they could see the Valley of Esdraelon with Mount Hermon in the distance. To the south they could see Jerusalem. What a view!

There they built a palace of ivory. Of course, the enemy in days gone by has carted away that beautiful ivory, but excavations have been going on there recently. In fact, Israel is excavating there now. Our guide told us that they have found several very delicate vessels of ivory. Apparently one of them was for perfume. The other vessels were probably for wine. Ivory was the color scheme of the palace, if you please.

Everything was done in ivory. Apparently, Ahab and Jezebel had the best interior decorator of the period come up and decorate for them. It was a palace of luxury.

God said He would destroy it and bring it to an end. I do not know of a more desolate spot today than the ruins of Samaria on top of that hill. I have many pictures that I took of it. God has certainly fulfilled that prophecy. Although we do not see prophecy which is being fulfilled in that land today, we can see that many prophecies have been fulfilled in the past. However, I repeat, that certainly the stage currently is being set for the fulfillment of future prophecies in the land of Palestine.

CHAPTER 4

THEME: Israel punished in past for iniquity

Beginning with this chapter, we have a series of three chapters which deal specifically with Israel, the ten tribes of the northern kingdom. In chapter 4 we will be reminded that God in the past punished Israel for iniquity. Then in chapter 5 we will see that in the future Israel will be punished for her iniquity. Finally, in chapter 6 we will see Amos admonishing his generation in the present to depart from iniquity. You see that this section has a very practical application to us as well as to Israel in the days of Amos.

As Amos is attempting to call the people back to God, he uses sarcasm that is really cutting.

> **Hear this word, ye kine of Bashan, that are in the mountain of Samaria, which oppress the poor, which crush the needy, which say to their masters, Bring, and let us drink [Amos 4:1].**

"Ye kine of Bashan"—kine are cows. Bashan is a territory on the east of the Jordan River between the mountains of Gilead in the south and Mount Hermon in the north. It was settled by the three tribes that stayed on the wrong side of Jordan, and it was part of the northern kingdom of Israel. It was a very fertile area and noted for its fine breed of cattle. The cows of Bashan were strong and sleek in appearance because of the lush grazing lands.

Now whom is Amos addressing? Who are the "cows of Bashan"? Because the word *cows* is feminine, some expositors believe he is speaking to the women who were living in luxury, well fed, well dressed, well groomed. To enable them to enjoy this wealth, the poor were oppressed. In fact, Amos says, "which oppress the poor, which crush the needy." Generally, a nation reveals its moral position and its economic standard by the way women dress. When women are well dressed and bejeweled, it denotes a time of affluence in the nation. So Amos could be referring to the women of Bashan.

However, I believe that Amos is speaking to the rulers. Why, then, does he use the feminine gender? Well, that crowd was homosexual. If you will read the first chapter of the Epistle to the Romans, you will see that homosexuality is a thing which God judges. We know from history that when a nation starts to go down, homosexuality comes to the forefront. It was that which began the downfall of Rome. Nero was a homosexual. Nero was known as a mad king. He was mad, yes, in a very unnatural way. In his great palace, he had one separate room which was reserved for the basest kind of sexual deviation imaginable. It was given over to the satisfying of his homosexual cravings. This certainly can be brought up to date. What is taking place in our own country is alarming, and it can spell our national doom. We need an Amos to speak out against the growing acceptance and even encouragement of homosexuality today.

> **The Lord God hath sworn by his holiness, that, lo, the days shall come upon you, that he will take you away with hooks, and your posterity with fishhooks [Amos 4:2].**

God uses the picture of having a hook in the jaw of the northern kingdom to drag them off into captivity. We sometimes speak of people being "hooked" on drugs. A person can be "hooked" by any besetting sin. God says these people are "hooked" for judgment. They are going to be dragged out of the land. We know from history that their conquerors did lead off their captives by a hook through the nose.

> **And ye shall go out at the breaches, every cow at that which is before her; and ye shall cast them into the palace, saith the Lord [Amos 4:3].**

In effect, God is saying, "If you think because you are rich or because you are a ruler living in a palace that you will be spared, you are wrong." And we read in the historical record that when Assyria finally came and took them into captivity, the king was taken also. This was true also of the southern kingdom when it went into Babylonia captivity.

Now we come to an arresting expression:

Come to Beth-el, and transgress; at Gilgal multiply transgression; and bring your sacrifices every morning, and your tithes after three years:

And offer a sacrifice of thanksgiving with leaven, and proclaim and publish the free offerings: for this liketh you, O ye children of Israel, saith the Lord GOD [Amos 4:4–5].

I am sure you recognize that Amos is using bitter sarcasm as he invites them to come up to Beth-el (the place where they went to worship the golden calf.) "Come to Beth-el, and transgress; at Gilgal multiply transgression." The word *Gilgal* means "circle, or to roll along." It was the first place to which Israel came after they had crossed the Jordan River under Joshua's leadership, and it became a sacred place to them. Later it became a center of idolatry, and here again it is associated with idolatry. So Amos invites them to "multiply transgression" at Gilgal. That would be saying today, "Come to church to sin." Obviously, one goes to church for the very opposite. Amos is using pungent satire and taunting rebuke. He makes such an ironical and ridiculous statement to alert the people as to what they are actually *doing.*

Do you know that sometimes it can actually be dangerous to go to church? The Devil goes to church, you know. I think that he gets up bright and early on a Sunday morning, and wherever there is the preaching and teaching of the Word of God, he is there trying to wreck their work in any way he can. That is the reason we ought to pray for Bible-preaching and Bible-teaching pastors. The Devil doesn't need to be busy in cults or in liberal churches which deny the Word of God. Those places are already in his domain. He must concentrate his efforts in those places where there is spiritual life and the Word of God is being given out.

When Jesus Christ was about to die and His enemies were plotting the details of His execution, He spent time in the Upper Room with His twelve disciples. You would think that was the most sacred spot in all the world at that moment. You might expect that the Devil was busy with those who were plotting the death of Jesus. But do you know where the Devil was that evening? He was in the Upper Room! He hadn't been invited, but he was there. Satan had entered into the heart of Judas Iscariot to betray Him, and he walked into the Upper Room on the legs of Judas. That's how he got there. And, my friend, sometimes he walks into our so-called conservative, fundamental churches on the legs of a deacon or a Sunday school teacher or another church member. It is tragic today to fail to recognize our enemy and to be ignorant of his devices.

In the days of Amos, the people of Israel were coming to the place of worship in a very pious manner. Amos indicates that they were offering a sacrifice of thanksgiving with leaven. If you are familiar with the Book of Leviticus, you may think it was strange that they used leaven in their offerings since in the Scriptures leaven represents evil—evil or wrong doctrine and evil living. In the Levitical system, at the Feast of Passover, the Feast of Unleavened Bread, and the Feast of Firstfruits, the use of leaven was forbidden. However, at the Feast of Pentecost, there was to be a meal offering to the Lord, which was to be presented in two loaves of fine flour baked *with leaven* (see Lev. 23). Pentecost was to depict the beginning and origin of the church. There has never yet been a church in which there wasn't at least a little leaven—that is, a little error or a little sin. For this reason leaven is included in the offering at Pentecost.

Also, leaven was used in the thanksgiving offerings. Leviticus 7 gives the law of the sacrifice of the peace offerings: "If he offer it for a thanksgiving, then he shall offer with the sacrifice of thanksgiving unleavened cakes mingled with oil, and unleavened wafers anointed with oil, and cakes mingled with oil, of fine flour, fried" (Lev. 7:12). This is the Godward side of the offering. You see, the Lord Jesus Christ has made peace with God for us. Because it represents Christ, there is no leaven in this first offering. In the New Testament this is made clear: "Therefore being justified by faith [not by works—we could never be justified by anything but faith], we have peace with God through our Lord Jesus Christ" (Rom. 5:1). Now, although the first offering represents Christ and contains no leaven, the second represents the manward side; the one who is bringing the sacrifice of thanksgiving offers *himself* to God: "Besides the cakes, he shall offer for his offering leavened bread with the sacrifice of thanksgiving of his peace offerings (Lev. 7:13).

We can make an application of this to our own lives. You and I can dedicate our lives to the Lord. Sometimes this is done in a ritual which is called a "consecration" service. Since the literal meaning of consecration is to set something apart as being holy, that is really a misnomer for that kind of ritual. We can never present ourselves holy or perfect before God. We will always contain some "leaven." So present yourself as a living sacrifice to God, as we are admonished in Romans 12:1. But don't ever think that you can present yourself *perfect* to God. If you are waiting for that before you feel you can present yourself to God, you will be waiting your whole lifetime.

Now, when Amos sarcastically invites the people of Israel to come to Beth-el and Gilgal to transgress, it is very significant that he tells them to "offer a sacrifice of thanksgiving with leaven." He doesn't even mention the first unleavened part of the offering. Why? Because the people are totally removed from the living and true God. Therefore, the only thing they can do is offer evil to God. Of course, God will not accept that at all. This prophet Amos, just a country preacher, has a lot on the ball! He is an outstanding minister of the Word of God. This is tremendous.

My friend, I hope you understand the satire and sarcasm of Amos when he invites people to Gilgal to transgress. He is not asking them to sin, but in biting sarcasm he is saying, "That's what you do when you come to Beth-el and to Gilgal. You come to *sin*, not to worship God!"

Next Sunday morning when you put on your Sunday-go-to-meeting clothes, it might be well to first get down on your knees and ask God about the condition of your heart. Will you be taking a clean heart to church? Will you be taking lips that will not speak anything to hurt the cause of Christ? The message of Amos is very pertinent even in our day. If Amos were still around and if I were still a pastor, I would invite him to my church to preach. I think the modern church needs ministers like him. There are many ministers who give only nice little messages on comfort and how to solve personal problems. Somebody needs to say something very strong about *sin* in people's hearts in our day. Sin is rampant in and out of the church, and it is rampant in your heart and in my heart this very day. The biggest problem you and I have is to overcome the sin which is in our lives. There is no use trying to cover it up by church attendance or by going to some little course or seminar. The essential thing is to have a confrontation with the Lord Jesus Christ and to get your relationship with Him straightened out.

Amos now reminds the people of Israel of the judgments God had sent upon them—

> **And I also have given you cleanness of teeth in all your cities, and want of bread in all your places: yet have ye not returned unto me, saith the LORD [Amos 4:6].**

They didn't have "cleanness of teeth" because God had given them a new toothpaste or new mouthwash! The reason they had clean teeth was that they had nothing to eat. God had judged them with famine, but it had not awakened them to their spiritual condition. "Yet have ye not returned unto me, saith the LORD." It made no impression on them.

> **And also I have withholden the rain from you, when there were yet three months to the harvest: and I caused it to rain upon one city, and caused it not to rain upon another city: one piece was rained upon, and the piece whereupon it rained not withered.**
>
> **So two or three cities wandered unto one city, to drink water; but they were not satisfied: yet have ye not returned unto me, saith the LORD [Amos 4:7–8].**

Then God sent a drought. God is the one who controls the rainfall— some think the weatherman does it! God withheld the rain three months before it was time to harvest, which was disastrous. And note that God caused it to rain on one city and not on another. God did this to show them that the rainfall was not by chance but by His sovereign will. The drought was so serious that people from one city would go to another city where there was water, and they would carry a little water home in a jug or wineskin. This should have turned them to God. "Yet have ye not returned unto me, saith the LORD."

Those of us from Texas can appreciate this. It was a three-year drought in West Texas that caused my Dad to leave there when I was a small boy. People in Dallas, Texas, can remember the drought that dried up the water supply for that city. They had to draw water from the Red River into which oil had been poured. I want to tell you, I have never tasted any other drinking water that was as bad as that! People who had friends or relatives in the little towns around Dallas would go there to fill up a jug of water to take it home for drinking. This wasn't new; it was the same thing the people were doing in the days of Amos. It was a warning from God, but they paid no attention to it.

> I have smitten you with blasting and mildew: when your gardens and your vineyards and your fig trees and your olive trees increased, the palmerworm devoured them: yet have ye not returned unto me, saith the LORD [Amos 4:9].

"Blasting and mildew." The crops were blasted by the scorching east wind from the desert, and the mildew was from excessive drought, not moisture. "The palmerworm devoured them" refers to a locust plague which devoured what was left. "Yet have ye not returned unto me, saith the LORD."

> I have sent among you the pestilence after the manner of Egypt: your young men have I slain with the sword, and have taken away your horses; and I have made the stink of your camps to come up unto your nostrils: yet have ye not returned unto me, saith the LORD [Amos 4:10].

"The stink of your camps" was the stench of the dead bodies from the pestilence and from the warfare. Yet with all of this, they did not return to the Lord!

> **I have overthrown some of you, as God overthrew Sodom and Gomorrah, and ye were as a firebrand plucked out of the burning: yet have ye not returned unto me, saith the LORD [Amos 4:11].**

Some Bible expositors feel that this is sort of a summation of the previous plagues. I rather doubt that because we know from the Book of Jonah that at this time the Assyrians were making forays down into the northern kingdom. Assyria would strike here and there and sometimes would take an entire community into captivity. God was permitting the Assyrian, just like a bird, to peck here and there in the kingdom. This should have been a warning to all the people that the whole kingdom might fall some day. They didn't accept the warning from God but continued on in their evil ways. "Yet have ye not returned unto me, saith the LORD."

> **Therefore thus will I do unto thee, O Israel: and because I will do this unto thee, prepare to meet thy God, O Israel [Amos 4:12].**

God does not tell them here what He is going to do. He simply says, "Thus will I do unto thee" and "because I will do this unto thee." It is going to be a surprise. We know now that it was the Assyrians who came down upon them suddenly and took them into captivity. In other words, the people of Israel simply did not believe God and did not turn to Him.

God goes even beyond the judgment of the Assyrian captivity. He says, "Prepare to meet thy God, O Israel." When Assyria came down, they didn't take all the people into captivity. Many of them were slain. This means that they were to meet God in death, which is something that every individual must do. We all must meet God in death. "Prepare to meet thy God, O Israel." This is a message to every individual even today.

God has dealt very definitely with a friend of mine because of the sin that was in his life. He told me the story of how God had dealt with him. The judgment that had come upon him was rather severe although it was something that a man could bear. As I was sympathizing with him about it, he said to me, "McGee, the judgment that has come upon me is not the thing that disturbs me. I have yet to stand before God, and I tremble."

I answered him, "You know that Vernon McGee is also going to stand before God. If I stood before Him as I am, I would be frightened to death. But I am not going to stand before Him as Vernon McGee. I am in Christ, and God is going to see Christ. I have been made acceptable in the Beloved." My friend answered, "Yes, that is the only comfort that I have for the life that I have lived."

Well, my friend, that message is for you also. Prepare to meet thy God. Suppose at this very moment you went into the presence of God—perhaps both you and I will be going there shortly. Suppose this life is past. The things that were so important to you down here will have no importance any more, I assure you. Life on earth is over, you're through, you're out of it, and you are in God's presence. How are you going to stand before Him? Perhaps you have lived to please people and have tried to keep up with the Joneses. Don't you know that you cannot stand in your own strength, your own life, your own character? You and I have nothing to offer to God—we are bankrupt, friend. We were *dead* in trespasses and sins. The only way you and I can stand there is in Christ. He "was delivered for our offences, and was raised again for our justification" (Rom. 4:25), that you and I might stand before Him justified. We stand before God in the righteousness of Christ.

Now our country preacher will tell us who this God is whom we are to meet. This is one of the most majestic awe-inspiring statements in the Word of God—

For, lo, he that formeth the mountains, and createth the wind, and declareth unto man what is his thought, that

**maketh the morning darkness, and treadeth upon the
high places of the earth, The LORD, The God of hosts, is
his name [Amos 4:13].**

Amos presents Him as the omnipotent, omniscient, and omnipresent
God. He is the omnipotent Creator. He has all power. It was He who
formed the mountains and created the wind. He is omniscient, knowing your thoughts afar off. And He is omnipresent—He "treadeth upon
the high places of the earth." No matter where you go, even to the
moon, you won't get away from Him, friend. Perhaps you have been
able to keep up a pretty good front so that your friends and neighbors
(and maybe even your mate) think you are a fine person. But in heaven,
the psalmist says, "Thou hast set our iniquities before thee, our secret
sins in the light of thy countenance" (Ps. 90:8). God knows you. There
is no use trying to keep up a front. You might as well go to Him and
turn yourself in. The FBI or the police may not be after you, but God
knows your transgressions. As Dr. Louis Sperry Chafer used to say to
us in class, secret sin on earth is open scandal in heaven. God not only
knows us through and through, but He also knew personally the people to whom Amos was speaking. With intensity of feeling Amos
urged them, "Prepare to meet thy God, O Israel."

CHAPTER 5

THEME: Israel will be punished in the future for iniquity

The previous chapter closed with a bang, with a note of finality. It would seem as if God had closed the door, that judgment was inevitable, and that there was no hope for Israel at all. Although chapter 5 reaches into the future and makes it very clear that God will punish them for their iniquity, in the first fifteen verses God pleads with Israel to seek Him so that judgment can be averted. As long as He did not bring that final stroke of judgment, their captivity, there was hope for them.

> **Hear ye this word which I take up against you, even a lamentation, O house of Israel [Amos 5:1].**

He is taking up a dirge. He is singing a funeral song, a very sad one. He speaks of them now with tenderness—

> **The virgin of Israel is fallen; she shall no more rise: she is forsaken upon her land; there is none to raise her up [Amos 5:2].**

When Hosea began his prophecy, he spoke of the experience he had had in his home. He had married a harlot, and God sent him out to speak to the northern kingdom, saying, "You're a harlot, but God still loves you." Here Amos says, "You were a virgin; God espoused you to Himself." That is the picture of every believer today. Paul said even to the Corinthians, "I espoused you as a chaste virgin to Christ" (see 2 Cor. 11:2). When we come to Him, our sins are forgiven and we start new with Him. But how about it, friend? How has it been going the past few years? Have you done what Israel did? Have you played the harlot? Have you turned away from the One who loves you? Have you been led astray into the world and into the things of the flesh? Is the Devil leading you around like a pig with a ring in its snout? A great many Christians are in that condition today. This is a sad funeral dirge: "The virgin of Israel is fallen; she shall no more rise: she is forsaken upon her land; there is none to raise her up."

For thus saith the Lord GOD; The city that went out by a thousand shall leave an hundred, and that which went forth by an hundred shall leave ten, to the house of Israel [Amos 5:3].

"The city that went out by a thousand shall leave an hundred." Amos is saying, "Prepare to meet your God. Look at the number that are going to be slain." "That which went forth by an hundred shall leave ten, to the house of Israel." These are the ones who will be left back in the land, but a great company of them will be slain.

Listen to Amos. This is, as it were, a last call to the nation—

For thus saith the LORD unto the house of Israel, Seek ye me, and ye shall live [Amos 5:4].

The invitation is still open. The Word has gone out. God is calling upon them to turn to Him; if they do even now, they will live.

But seek not Beth-el, nor enter into Gilgal, and pass not to Beer-sheba: for Gilgal shall surely go into captivity, and Beth-el shall come to nought [Amos 5:5].

"But seek not Beth-el." Beth-el is where one of the golden calves was erected. By the way, you cannot find Beth-el today. I have had two different spots pointed out to me by guides, so we cannot be sure just where it is. The general location is pretty well known, but to be able to pinpoint it seems to be a problem.

"Nor enter into Gilgal." Gilgal is the place where Israel camped when they crossed the Jordan River when they first came into the land under the leadership of Joshua. There they set up the tabernacle, and there was the staging area for their march upon Jericho. It became a very sacred place. In fact, God had told them to tell their children that that was the place where He had delivered them. Instead, these people had gone into idolatry, and these places that had been sacred for God became places to set up an idol.

"And pass not to Beer-sheba." Beer-sheba was way down in the southern kingdom of Judah in the Negeb. It is another very famous place. It was at Beer-sheba that Abraham and Abimelech made a covenant, and then Abraham called on the name of the Lord (see Gen. 21). The expression, ". . . from Dan to Beer-sheba . . ." (e.g., see Jud. 20:1), is used in Scripture to designate the whole land of Israel from north to south. In the days of Amos, the people in the northern kingdom were making pilgrimages to Beer-sheba for the worship of idols.

"For Gilgal shall surely go into captivity, and Beth-el shall come to nought." Why doesn't Amos mention Beer-sheba at this point? Because Beer-sheba is not in the northern kingdom but in the southern. It will be more than another hundred years before Beer-sheba goes into captivity with the southern kingdom. However, these two in the northern kingdom, both Beth-el and Gilgal, are about to go into captivity. How accurate Amos is in his statement here!

But he goes on to say that there is still hope for them—

> **Seek the Lord, and ye shall live; lest he break out like fire in the house of Joseph, and devour it, and there be none to quench it in Beth-el [Amos 5:6].**

"Seek the Lord, and ye shall live"—what a wonderful invitation this is! "Lest he break out like fire in the house of Joseph." God says, "If you do not turn to Me, I will have to judge you."

> **Ye who turn judgment to wormwood, and leave off righteousness in the earth [Amos 5:7].**

The man who was liberal in his theology used to make a great deal of this section of Scripture. He presented a "works salvation," finding justification for it in this passage. Unfortunately, he did not consider

Amos' entire message. The condition of the people of Israel was that they were going through the *form* of worship that God had prescribed. They were offering sacrifices, they were going through a ritual that God had given to them, but their lives did not commend their profession. In other words, their practice did not equal the profession which they made.

Years ago Dr. G. Campbell Morgan said that he was more afraid of the blasphemy of the secular than he was of the blasphemy of the sanctuary. Many people think that if you participate in all the forms and rituals of the church, you are very pious, but if you do something in the sanctuary which is not according to the ritual of the church, it is blasphemous. My friend, I do not feel that the real danger is in that sort of thing. The real danger is in the man who goes to church and sings the doxology, "Praise God from whom all blessings flow," but outside the church is living a life in which he is not honest and a life in which there is neither justice nor righteousness. That is the blasphemy of the secular or the blasphemy of the street. *That* is the thing that God is condemning in the lives of the people of Israel.

I am not saying that a living faith in Christ is not essential. It is absolutely essential to trust in Christ for your salvation. But, my friend, if you make a profession of trusting in Christ and your life outside the church does not commend the Gospel at all, then, may I say to you, there is not but one word to describe that. It is a harsh word, but the Lord Jesus is the one who used this word more than anyone else. He called the religious rulers of His day, "Ye *hypocrites*." That is His word for it—I did not think of it. It is brazen hypocrisy today, either in the pulpit or in the pew, when a profession is given and a protestation is made of our wonderful love for and trust in Christ, and then we go out and live a life which condemns the very Gospel we are supposed to be professing. This is the thing that hurts the cause of the Gospel today. A great many Christians do not want this mentioned because they are very active in Christian work but not very active in living for the Lord in their business and social lives.

I knew a man who was married and very active in the church; I do not think there was an organization within the church in which he was not active. But he got involved with a lady in the choir. He dropped out for a time, and without making any amends, without any apparent change of life whatsoever, he wanted to come back into active service in the church. As pastor, I absolutely condemned that sort of thing, and I was made out to be the unreasonable party because of it.

Amos condemns this idea of making a profession and then not living up to it—this was basic in his message. You see, God had to bring Amos from way down south in the southern kingdom in order to get a man who would give this kind of message. The paid preachers up there in Beth-el and Samaria were saying only what the people wanted them to say.

A leading Bible expositor made the statement several years ago that the modern pulpit had become a sounding board for the thinking of the congregation. Paul wrote to Timothy, "For the time will come when they will not endure sound doctrine; but after their own lusts shall they heap to themselves teachers, having itching ears; And they shall turn away their ears from the truth, and shall be turned unto fables" (2 Tim. 4:3-4). The people's ears itch to hear something nice and sweet, and then they go up and pat the preacher on the back, telling him how sweet he is. It becomes like the old Egyptian game: "You scratch my back, I'll scratch your back, and we both will have a good time." A great deal of that type of thing is going on in our churches today; liberalism has done it for years, and we find it in many conservative churches today.

The people of Israel were insulted that this man Amos would even suggest that they were not very religious or very pious, but that was his message to them.

> **Seek him that maketh the seven stars and Orion, and turneth the shadow of death into the morning, and maketh the day dark with night: that calleth for the waters of the sea, and poureth them out upon the face of the earth: The Lord is his name [Amos 5:8].**

Again, this is God's gracious call. God is long-suffering. God is much more patient than I would be. I have found out that I need to learn to be patient with the patience of God. How long-suffering and patient He is

"Seek him that maketh the seven stars and Orion." Orion is one of the many constellations in the heavens, and it was the one, of course, familiar to these people in that day.

"And maketh the day dark with night: that calleth for the waters of the sea, and poureth them out upon the face of the earth." That is, it is God who makes the rain fall. It is true that rainfall is controlled by the law of hydrodynamics, but who made the law of hydrodynamics? Who is the One who pulls the water up out of the ocean, puts it on the train (they call it a cloud), moves those clouds with the wind until they get to just the right place, then turns loose the rain? God is the One doing that, my friend. Amos says, "The LORD is his name." In effect, he is saying to the people of Israel, "You have turned to idols, and your life does not commend your profession of a faith in the living God, the living God who is the Creator."

> **That strengtheneth the spoiled against the strong, so that the spoiled shall come against the fortress.**
>
> **They hate him that rebuketh in the gate, and they abhor him that speaketh uprightly [Amos 5:9–10].**

"They hate him that rebuketh in the gate." The one who rebuketh in the gate would be a judge. The courthouse of that day was the gate of the walled city. You will find all the way through Scripture that the judges sat in the gate. Boaz brought the nearer kinsman to the gate of Bethlehem to settle the inheritance of Naomi and Ruth. When Lot went down to Sodom, he became involved in politics down there, and we are told that he sat in the gate. What was he doing there? He was a judge. Amos says that the judge who rebuked that which was wrong was the one who was hated; therefore, most of the judges chose to cooperate with the evildoers.

"And they abhor him that speaketh uprightly." When a judge insisted upon justice and upon that which was right, he became very unpopular. I am not sure that human nature has changed very much since Amos' day.

> Forasmuch therefore as your treading is upon the poor,
> and ye take from him burdens of wheat: ye have built
> houses of hewn stone, but ye shall not dwell in them; ye
> have planted pleasant vineyards, but ye shall not drink
> wine of them [Amos 5:11].

"Forasmuch therefore as your treading is upon the poor, and ye take from him burdens of wheat." The poor are the ones who do not get justice. I know that, for I have been on that side of the line for a long time.

"Ye have built houses of hewn stone, but ye shall not dwell in them; ye have planted pleasant vineyards, but ye shall not drink wine of them." The beautiful palaces that were built at Samaria are in ruins today. They were destroyed shortly after this message was given and have been in ruins now for nearly three thousand years.

> For I know your manifold transgressions, and your
> mighty sins: they afflict the just, they take a bribe, and
> they turn aside the poor in the gate from their right
> [Amos 5:12].

The poor could not get justice in the court of that day. Has it changed today?

One of the reasons offered for repealing the death penalty has been that the rich man can always escape the gas chamber or the electric chair. I do not think that is a legitimate reason although it is true that the rich man can do that. The poor man, when he is found guilty, does not stand a chance of escaping the penalty. The rich man can keep appealing the case, and it takes him a long time to find his way to jail; in fact, in many cases, he never even gets there.

God takes notice when there is no justice in a nation. God has turned over to human government the responsibility of running this earth. The nations of the earth are God's arrangement, and He holds them accountable. When they fail, He removes them, as Rome was removed from the scene.

**Therefore the prudent shall keep silence in that time; for
it is an evil time [Amos 5:13].**

In other words, a man in that day knew he could not get justice, and
many good people were keeping quiet. It was the prudent thing to do
because, if he had attempted to protest, it wouldn't have done him a bit
of good. The tragedy of the hour in which we live is that we talk about
the freedom of the press, the freedom of religion, and the freedom of
speech, but there is not much of it left. The news media have definitely
become a brainwashing agency. It is true that only he who has money
can get a public hearing today. As a result, we do have a silent majority
in this country because they know that their voices would not amount
to anything at all. We are in a tragic day, very much like the day to
which Israel had come.

**Seek good, and not evil, that ye may live: and so the
LORD, the God of hosts, shall be with you, as ye have
spoken [Amos 5:14].**

Again, the Lord calls upon Israel to turn to Him.

**Hate the evil, and love the good, and establish judgment
in the gate: it may be that the LORD God of hosts will be
gracious unto the remnant of Joseph [Amos 5:15].**

In our day, a man who is liberal and supported by some rich organization can betray our government and escape any penalty (in fact, he is
even made a hero) while some poor fellow who is espousing an honest
cause does not stand a chance of gaining a hearing. God says, "Hate
the evil, and love the good, and establish judgment in the gate."

"It may be that the LORD God of hosts will be gracious unto the
remnant of Joseph." In other words, Amos says, "It's a slim chance, but
there is hope for you."

Now Amos moves into another area, the warning of an approaching
judgment, the Day of the Lord.

Therefore the LORD, the God of hosts, the Lord, saith thus; Wailing shall be in all streets; and they shall say in all the highways, Alas! alas! and they shall call the husbandman to mourning, and such as are skilful of lamentation to wailing.

And in all vineyards shall be wailing: for I will pass through thee, saith the LORD [Amos 5:16-17].

Because God knew that they would not repent, He now clearly states the judgment which is to come. Death will touch everyone; all will mourn.

Woe unto you that desire the day of the LORD! to what end is it for you? the day of the LORD is darkness, and not light [Amos 5:18].

A great many people were very piously saying that they desired the Day of the Lord. Amos expresses it here as a "Woe"—"Woe unto you that desire the day of the LORD!" But for them it is nothing in the world but pious sentiment. That day is not going to be as pleasant for them as they think it is going to be.

Amos uses here the expression, "the day of the LORD." Joel is the one who introduced this subject in prophecy, and every one of the prophets after him has something to say about it. Many people have thought that the Day of the Lord refers to the Millennium; in fact, at the beginning of my theological training that is what I was taught. Joel was very careful (and Amos will be also) to say that the Day of the Lord is not light but it is darkness. The Day of the Lord begins with judgment and moves on to the coming of Christ to establish His kingdom here upon this earth.

There are a number of commentators who feel that the people of Israel were becoming rather cynical and were ridiculing the Day of the Lord. I do not see that here at all; I do not see how the interpretation could possibly be true. Rather, I see that the people were becoming very pious. They were going through the Mosaic rituals, but they were also worshipping idols. It was just religion to them, just as churchgoing is to many people today. There is nothing vital, nothing real in going through a ritual. The reason many church services are so dead is that they are nothing more than ritual. It may be beautiful, it may appeal to your eyes and your ears, but does it change your life? Is it transforming? Is it something you can live by in the marketplace? There are many people today who are premillennial and pretribulational in their theology and who very piously say, "Oh, if only the Lord would come!" If you are one of them, let me ask you this: Do you really want Him to come? Or are you using the Rapture of the church as a sort of an escape mechanism to get you out of your troubles down here?

In seminary a fellow student and I were studying Hebrew. After dinner in the evening, when we had a difficult Hebrew assignment to prepare for the next day, he would look up to the heavens and say, "Oh, if the Lord would only come tonight!" What was he after? He didn't want to study Hebrew! But I never shall forget the night before graduation (he was to be married and go on his honeymoon the day after graduation) when he came out of the cafeteria, looked up to the sky, and said, "I sure hope the Lord doesn't come now for several days!" My friend, many of us look forward to the Rapture, not because we love Christ's appearing, but because we want to escape an unpleasant situation.

Amos says to these people, "You pious folk are just going through the religious rituals, you don't really know God—you are worshipping idols also! The Day of the Lord is not something which you are to desire. It is not light, but it is a day of darkness. You will first go through a great period of tribulation when the Day of the Lord comes. What you expect to do is to jump right into the Millennium, but that is not the way it is going to happen.

Those of us who believe that the church will not go through the Tribulation should be aware that we will not escape all judgment. My friend, some of us may think we have gotten into the Tribulation after we get to heaven! Do you know why? Listen to what Paul has to say in 2 Corinthians 5:9–10: "Wherefore we labour, that, whether present or absent, we may be accepted of him. For we must all appear before the judgment seat of Christ; that every one may receive the things done in

his body, according to that he hath done, whether it be good or bad."
The judgment seat of Christ is the *bema;* it is not the Great White
Throne judgment at all. It is to the *bema* that all Christians come "that
every one may receive the things done in his body, according to that he
hath done, whether it be good or bad." Is this a judgment for salvation?
No, Paul says, "For other foundation can no man lay than that is laid,
which is Jesus Christ" (1 Cor. 3:11). There is no other foundation any
man can lay, but you can build on that foundation. You can build with
wood, hay, and stubble; or you can build with gold, silver, and precious stones. But every man's *work*—not his salvation, not his
person—will be tested by fire. If any man's work survives the fire, he
will receive a reward. But suppose his work does not survive the fire?
Paul says, "He himself shall be saved; yet so as by fire" (see 1 Cor.
3:12–15). This is the reason I often make the statement that although
many people are saved, they are going to smell like they were bought at
a fire sale when they get to heaven. Everything they did here on earth,
they did in the flesh, they did it for some earthly reason, for some
present satisfaction.

I want to be very frank with you: as I am now getting toward the
sunset of life, I'm wondering how Vernon McGee is going to fare at the
judgment seat of Christ. You may say that I will get a reward because of
my Bible-teaching ministry through the years. But you don't know me
like I know myself; if you did, you might not want to listen to me. But
wait a minute, don't put the book down, because if I knew you like you
know yourself, I wouldn't want to talk to you.

My friend, the lives which we live down here are to be *tested,* and it
is pious nonsense to pretend to be so interested in the coming of Christ
when the truth is that some of us will get to heaven and think that we
didn't miss the Great Tribulation after all. Notice what Paul went on to
say after speaking of our judgment at the *bema* of Christ: "Knowing
therefore the terror of the Lord, we persuade men . . ." (2 Cor. 5:11). If
you think that when you appear in His presence He is going to give
you a nice little Sunday school medal because you didn't miss Sunday
school for fifteen years, I think you are wrong. I do not think that
is even going to be an issue. I think that the life you live in your home,
your witness in your business and social life, your conduct with the

opposite sex are the things which are going to come before the judgment seat of Christ—it will be the things that were done in the body down here.

Do you want to go to heaven now? Do you have everything straightened out? Paul writes, "For if we would judge ourselves, we should not be judged" (1 Cor. 11:31). This is the reason I try to keep everything confessed to the Lord. I want to run short accounts with Him every day. If I don't, He is going to straighten it out up there someday. You lost your temper and gave a poor witness today. Or you gossiped about another believer. Do you think that when you come into the presence of Christ He will pat you on the back and say what a nice little fellow you were? He is going to judge those things, my friend. Things must be made right in heaven, and that is the purpose of the judgment seat of Christ.

Amos is really putting it on the line to these people. He says, "Cut out this nonsense that you desire the Day of the Lord. It is not a day of light but of darkness. There will be a Great Tribulation that you will go through." If you are a believer and therefore do not go through that, there will still be the judgment seat of Christ for you. I do not think that it is going to be as pleasant as some folk think it is going to be.

As if a man did flee from a lion, and a bear met him; or went into the house, and leaned his hand on the wall, and a serpent bit him [Amos 5:19].

Amos is one of the most dramatic preachers that you will find in Scripture. He uses such figurative language. He uses the idiom of the earth and draws his illustrations from nature. Here he describes a man who is out in the woods, and suddenly there is a lion on the trail in back of him. As he runs away from the lion, he sees a bear coming toward him. In other words, if you say you want the Lord to come so that you can get out of your troubles down here, it may be like jumping out of the frying pan into the fire (to use an adage of our day). Seeing the bear coming toward him, the man takes off over the hill and reaches his home. He puts his hand upon the wall to rest and get his breath, only to have a serpent come out of the wall and bite him. It might have been better if the lion or the bear had gotten him than to have the poison of a serpent in him!

Amos is saying that we had better be very careful about the life we are living for God down here. As believers, our *salvation* is not in jeopardy—Christ has paid the penalty for our sins, but if our sins as believers are not dealt with and made right, *He* will make them right. My friend, He *must* do that—He is holy and righteous and just, and heaven is a place where things are right. Therefore, you and I will have to be right when we get there. This is something that a great many people do not realize today.

> **Shall not the day of the LORD be darkness, and not light? even very dark, and no brightness in it? [Amos 5:20].**

"The day of the LORD" begins with a period of judgment that is yet to come upon the nation of Israel. There is more than a period of judgment that is included in the Day of the Lord, however. The Day of the Lord also includes the second coming of Christ to the earth and the time of the millennial kingdom here upon earth.

> **I hate, I despise your feast days, and I will not smell in your solemn assemblies.**
>
> **Though ye offer me burnt offerings and your meat offerings, I will not accept them: neither will I regard the peace offerings of your fat beasts.**
>
> **Take thou away from me the noise of thy songs; for I will not hear the melody of thy viols [Amos 5:21-23].**

Behind their going through the rituals were lives that were dishonest. God's people need to recognize that their faith must be real. Faith is not fake or fable; it is reality. Faith must lay hold of a person. Believing is not deceiving. Many people say, "If you believe, it is because you are blind. You have a blind faith." My friend, if it is a blind faith, forget it because God does not accept that. Faith must have an effect upon the life; James says, ". . . faith without works is dead?" (James 2:20). Paul said that we have been saved in order that we might produce good works. All of this is important.

The people of Israel were living lives of sin. They were engaged in idolatry; yet they were going through all the Mosaic ritual. God says here, "I despise it. I have no use for it." In some of our song services which we consider to be so enthusiastic, if the hearts of the people are not in it, if there is nothing but a big mouth in it, do you really think God accepts that? If He came to your church or my church, what do you think His viewpoint would be?

> **But let judgment run down as waters, and righteousness as a mighty stream.**
>
> **Have ye offered unto me sacrifices and offerings in the wilderness forty years, O house of Israel?**
>
> **But ye have borne the tabernacle of your Moloch and Chiun your images, the star of your god, which ye made to yourselves [Amos 5:24–26].**

Apparently, the people of Israel offered sacrifices in the wilderness, but when they met a heathen people, they wanted to take on the worship of their gods also. The worship of Moloch was that in which small children were put into the arms of a red-hot idol and made human sacrifices. The screams of these children were terrible. God is saying to us, "You come to church on Sunday and go through the motions of worshipping Me, but during the week you worship Moloch, you worship the idol of covetousness as you go after the almighty dollar."

Cardinal Wolsey was banished from Hampton Court by Henry VIII who would also have had him executed if Wolsey had not died a natural death before the execution could take place. On his deathbed, the cardinal said, "If I had only served my God like I served my king!" Many a Christian will have to say on his deathbed, "I have served the god of Moloch down here; I have served the idol of covetousness. I've worshipped the things of the flesh and have not served my God." My friend, it does not matter how sweet the music will be, nor what nice words the preacher will say at the funeral, you and I are going to stand at the judgment seat of Christ. I will be frank with you, that disturbs me somewhat. Therefore, I want to keep things straightened out with Him down here.

> **Therefore will I cause you to go into captivity beyond Damascus, saith the LORD, whose name is The God of hosts [Amos 5:27].**

Israel is to be punished in the future. They will go into captivity "beyond Damascus" (that is, beyond Syria), and beyond Damascus was Nineveh. God is telling Israel that the Assyrian would take them into captivity.

CHAPTER 6

THEME: Israel admonished in the present to depart from iniquity

Amos begins this chapter with a "Woe." He is not a prophet who majors in woes, but you will find them in several other of the prophets and in the Book of Revelation. "Woe" also means "Whoa!"— it means to stop, look, and listen because this is something that is important. The word *woe* is one that ought to draw our special attention to that which follows.

> **Woe to them that are at ease in Zion, and trust in the mountain of Samaria, which are named chief of the nations, to whom the house of Israel came! [Amos 6:1].**

Zion was, of course, in the southern kingdom of Judah; so both parts of the nation, Judah and Israel, are addressed here. Zion was the center of religion—God's temple was there, and Samaria was the metropolis of a powerful kingdom.

"Woe to them that are at ease in Zion." The common expression at departure a few years ago was, "Well, take it easy!" Today we often say, "Have a good day!" which I take to mean practically the same thing. That is what Israel was doing: they were taking it easy. "Woe to them that are at ease in Zion." They were sitting in the lap of luxury in a day of affluence. We have been doing that as a nation since the depression and World War II—we have been sitting in the lap of luxury in a day of affluence.

"And trust in the mountain of Samaria." It was as if Samaria was the place where they stored their atom bombs. It was the capital of the northern kingdom, Ahab and Jezebel had lived there, and lovely palaces of ivory were built there. The mountains of Samaria provided such excellent natural fortifications that the city was able to stand the Assyrian siege for three years before it fell. Samaria was such an important city that after the Assyrians had destroyed it, Herod later rebuilt it. Herod was quite a builder, and he built all over Palestine. He built Caesarea right from the ground up, but Samaria he rebuilt because it was such a marvelous location. With all this luxury and excellent fortifications, Israel felt secure and well protected.

"Which are named chief of the nations, to whom the house of Israel came!" "Chief of the nations" probably refers to Israel's princes who were men of rank and authority. To these godless and careless heads of the nation the people of Israel came for justice and for help. But the princes were interested only in their own ease and self-indulgence. The term *chief of the nations* may also refer to Israel herself, as she was recognized among the nations in that day. In other words, she belonged to the United Nations and had a great deal of influence.

> **Pass ye unto Calneh, and see; and from thence go ye to Hamath the great: then go down to Gath of the Philistines: be they better than these kingdoms? or their border greater than your border? [Amos 6:2].**

"Pass ye unto Calneh, and see." Calneh is one of the cities that was in the intersection of the Tigris River and the upper Zab River. Nineveh was there, Calneh was there, and that area constituted a great center.

"And from thence go ye to Hamath the great." Hamath is the chief city in Syria. We are going south now.

"Then go down to Gath of the Philistines." Gath is way south in Philistia and was the leading city of the Philistines.

"Be they better than these kingdoms? or their border greater than you border?" In other words, "Go look at these other nations. Why do you think that you are superior to these nations? You're not superior. You are engaged in the same sins that they are, and your responsibility is greater. They have no revelation from God, but you do have a revelation from God."

Now Amos will mention the three national sins of Israel. These are the three sins which brought the northern kingdom down. They also brought Babylon down; they brought Egypt down; they brought Greece down; and they brought Rome down. They have brought down

many great nations. They are the reason that France and Great Britain
have become second-rate nations today. At one time we said, "The sun
never sets on the British Empire," but today it looks as if the British
Empire itself is setting. These three sins are national sins, and they are
sins for which God will judge the nations.

**Ye that put far away the evil day, and cause the seat of
violence to come near [Amos 6:3].**

Israel was saying, "Yes, a day of judgment is coming, but it is not near.
We do not need to worry about it." That was the thing that Hezekiah
said to Isaiah when Isaiah told him that judgment was coming on the
southern kingdom and that they were to be carried into captivity. Hezekiah said, "Will it be in my day?" Isaiah said, "No, it won't be in your
day." And even Hezekiah, who was a great king, said, "Well, then,
that's all right."

Our present generation is passing on to our grandchildren a nation
that is in debt and in great trouble. I used to worry about my daughter
and the day in which she would live. Now I worry about my two little
grandsons and the world that they are moving into and in which they
will live. The evil day is coming.

What are the three sins which destroy a nation? The first sin is
given in verse 4—

**That lie upon beds of ivory, and stretch themselves upon
their couches, and eat the lambs out of the flock, and the
calves out of the midst of the stall [Amos 6:4].**

Illicit sex and gluttony are the two sins that are mentioned here, and
they are sins of the flesh.

"That lie upon beds of ivory." Ahab and Jezebel had built an ivory
palace in Samaria. It has been thoroughly excavated now, and the
workmen have found there many very fine, delicate vessels that were
in the rubble and ruin of that great palace. That palace represented the
life of the upper class of that day. "They lie upon beds of ivory"—they
all had king-sized beds. They were taking it easy.

"And stretch themselves upon their couches" suggests their preoccupation with sex. That was the thing that they were engaged in, and it is that which characterizes our own day. Someone tried to answer the current women's liberation movement by saying that the woman's place is in the kitchen and in the bedroom. May I say to you, that is an awful thing to say. I totally disagree with that comment, but it does show the color and complexion of our nation today. Much has been reported in the press regarding the social life in our nation's capital. We are told that when they get together, they are heavily involved in drinking and that the main topic of conversation is who is dating whose wife. Such activity is not limited to those of any particular political party. Thank God there are individuals who are exceptions to this type of thing, but I am afraid that more attention is paid to sex in Washington, D.C., than to any of the problems which face this nation. When our lawmakers appear on television, they become very serious, but their social life—this is not true of all of them, of course—seems to be very corrupt.

No nation has been able to survive such involvement in sin. Rome was probably the greatest of all nations; then why did it fall apart? No outside enemy destroyed Rome. It was like "Humpty-Dumpty"—

> Humpty-Dumpty sat on a wall,
> Humpty-Dumpty had a great fall;
> All the King's horses, and all the King's men
> Could not put Humpty-Dumpty together again.

Why did Rome fall? Gibbon, in his *Decline and Fall of the Roman Empire*, mentions that the destruction of the family was one of the important reasons Rome fell. When immorality came in, then the nation began to go down.

The second national sin is given in verse 5—

That chant to the sound of the viol, and invent to themselves instruments of music, like David [Amos 6:5].

They came up with a lot of new tunes in that day. You may think that jazz, rock and roll, and hard rock music are something new, but Israel had it back in that day. The character of music can destroy a nation, and as far as I'm concerned, we have arrived at that point in our nation. I know that I sound like a square and a real backward fellow, and that I am. Someone will say, "You just don't know anything about music." While it is true that I do not know much about music, I do know what I like and what I don't like; a lot of it I don't like today, and I simply do not listen to it.

"They chant to the sound of the viol, and invent to themselves instruments of music, like David." But the music was no longer used as it was in David's day. David was a genius whose music was to praise and glorify God. Israel also had geniuses in Amos' day, but they were not writing music to the praise and glory of God. Instead, it was that which took people away from God and from the worship of God.

Now we come to the third national sin—

That drink wine in bowls, and anoint themselves with the chief ointments: but they are not grieved for the affliction of Joseph [Amos 6:6].

"That drink wine in bowls"—not just in little glasses but in bowls; they were really alcoholics.

"And anoint themselves with the chief ointments: but they are not grieved for the affliction of Joseph." In that day there was a great deal of attention given to the matter of getting the right kind of ointment for the underarms. I don't mind mentioning this because it is mentioned on television all the time. It was pretty important in Israel that you use the right kind of deodorant, but it was drunkenness that was destroying the nation.

Drunkenness is the thing that is destroying our nation today along with these other sins—and we are not getting by with it, my friend. There is an alarming number of alcoholics in this country and many, many more people whose lives are directly affected by the alcoholic. A majority of the fatal automobile accidents are caused by alcohol. More people are being killed in automobile accidents in this country than were ever killed in Vietnam, but no one is protesting about that.

I was amazed a few years ago when one of the distilleries ran an

advertisement about young people drinking, saying they were concerned about the problem. In their ad, they said: "Teenagers, especially in a group, are often tempted to do things they might not do on
their own, like taking a drink when they know they shouldn't. We are
sure you are concerned about this problem." Imagine the liquor
makers telling you and me that they think we are concerned because
they are concerned! Well, why don't they quit making the stuff? Their
ad continued: "You don't have to worry much about it if you've shown
your youngster over the years that your ideas about drinking are
healthy and mature." What are "healthy and mature" ideas about
drinking? Drinking is drinking, isn't it? They certainly were not running an advertisement for prohibition!

I would like to share with you this poem, "It's Nobody's
Business"—

> It's nobody's business what I drink.
> I care not what my neighbors think,
> Or how many laws they choose to pass.
> I'll tell the world I'll have my glass.
> Here's one man's freedom cannot be curbed.
> My right to drink is undisturbed.
> So he drank in spite of law or man,
> Then got into his old tin can,
> Stepped on the gas and let it go,
> Down the highway to and fro.
> He took the curves at fifty miles,
> With bleary eyes and a drunken smile.
> Not long 'til a car he tried to pass,
> Then a crash, a scream, and breaking glass.
> The other car was upside down,
> About two miles from the nearest town.
> The man was clear, but his wife was caught,
> And he needed the help of that drunken sot,
> Who sat in a mauldin, drunken daze
> And heard the scream and saw the blaze,
> But too far gone to save a life.

By helping the car from off the wife.
The car was burned and a mother died,
While a husband wept and a baby cried.
And a drunk sat by, and still some think
It's nobody's business what they drink.

—Unknown

The sins of the flesh (illicit sex and gluttony), heathen music, and drunkenness are the three great sins which have brought great nations down. I simply cannot believe that our nation will be the exception to the rule. It is enough to break any person's heart to see what is happening in this great nation of ours. Yet we try to explain it away by saying that now we are civilized, now we have a new morality, now we have grown up and gotten rid of the old Puritan notions. By the way, the Puritans and the Pilgrims founded a great nation. Are we, the sophisticated and suave folk, going to keep that great nation, or are we losing it?

This message from Amos was fulfilled in his day. The northern kingdom was destroyed and went into captivity. These are the sins that brought it down. In verse 4 it was gluttony and illicit sex; in verse 5 it was heathen music; and in verse 6 it was drunkenness. It is the same old story: wine, women, and song. That is what a great many people think life is all about. Actually, that is not what life is all about but what death is all about. It is the philosophy which says, "Eat, drink, and be merry, for tomorrow we die." Or the philosophy which says, "Pick the daisies while you can"—the day is coming when you won't be able to pick them. In other words, satisfy self. But if a man (or a nation) goes down that line, he will find out that it does not lead to a pot of gold; it is a dead-end street with the emphasis upon *dead*. It has led to the death of individuals and of nations.

All of this reveals something quite interesting about the human heart. You can put the whole world into the heart, and it still will not be satisfied. That is remarkable, is it not? Only God can fill the vacuum of the human heart. The iniquity of Israel is going to lead to the destruction of the nation—

**Therefore now shall they go captive with the first that go
captive, and the banquet of them that stretched themselves shall be removed [Amos 6:7].**

"Therefore." One preacher has said that when you come to *therefore* in
the Bible, you'd better investigate what it's there for. Here it leads to
this great statement that because of these three great sins, the northern kingdom will go into captivity first. That is the direction in which
they were moving, and they were moving rapidly. They were much
closer to it than they could really believe.

**The Lord God hath sworn by himself, saith the Lord the
God of hosts, I abhor the excellency of Jacob, and hate
his palaces: therefore will I deliver up the city with all
that is therein [Amos 6:8].**

Their palaces were places of corruption and storehouses of plunder
from the poor. God hated all this. If you want to know God's attitude
toward the present-day philosophy of the new morality, of illicit sex,
gluttony, degrading music, and drunkenness, He makes it very clear
here. God says He *hates* them. As a result of these sins, Israel had
become a godless nation. These are the things which will take you
away from God or prevent your coming to Him in the first place.

**And it shall come to pass, if there remain ten men in one
house, that they shall die [Amos 6:9].**

Some expositors believe that this refers to the coming of a devastating
plague, such as often follows warfare.

**And a man's uncle shall take him up, and he that
burneth him, to bring out the bones out of the house,
and shall say unto him that is by the sides of the house,
Is there yet any with thee? and he shall say, No. Then
shall he say, Hold thy tongue: for we may not make mention of the name of the Lord [Amos 6:10].**

This is a strange statement. I shall give you Dr. Charles L. Feinberg's explanation (from his book *Joel, Amos and Obadiah* pp. 89–90), which is probably accurate:

> How widespread the plague will be is noted for us in verse 10. When one's next of kin, to whom the duty of burial belonged, would come to carry the corpse out of the house to burn it, he would find but one remaining out of the ten who lived there formerly. And that last surviving one hidden away in the innermost recesses of the houses fearfully awaiting the hour when the plague would carry him away also. In ancient Israel in accordance with the words of Genesis 3:19 burial was the accepted method of disposal of the dead. In this the New Testament doctrine of the body concurs. Hence cremation was considered wrong and not countenanced (see Amos 2:1). But when God's judgment falls upon His people, there will be so many dead that they will not bury but burn them. The cases here and 1 Samuel 31:12 are exceptional cases. Here cremation is resorted to in order to prevent contagion; in 1 Samuel it was done to obviate further dishonor of the bodies of Saul and his sons by the Philistines. When asked if there are others alive, the remaining occupant of the house will say there is none. Immediately he will be told to hold his peace for fear he would mention the name of the Lord in announcing the death of the others in the household, or in praising God for his own deliverance. Punishment will so work fear and despair in them all that they will refrain from even the mention of the name of the Lord (which should be their sole refuge in such an hour) lest further wrath come upon them.

> **For, behold, the Lord commandeth, and he will smite the great house with breaches, and the little house with clefts [Amos 6:11].**

High and low, great and small were going into Assyrian captivity.

**Shall horses run upon the rock? will one plow there
with oxen? for ye have turned judgment into gall, and
the fruit of righteousness into hemlock [Amos 6:12].**

"Shall horses run upon the rock?" If you have ever ridden horseback in
mountain country where there is great deal of rock, you know that a
horse can slip and fall there. As a young fellow I belonged to the cav-
alry division of the National Guard. We were out on patrol duty, and I
was riding a big, tall, red horse. The section I patrolled was a very
rocky one up in middle Tennessee. My horse slipped and fell on one of
my feet. As a result, I got out of patrol duty and was sent home because
they did not want me hanging around. That got me out of a lot of hard
work, and very frankly, I have always appreciated that old red horse.
"Shall horses run upon the rock?" Well, they'd better not because they
will slip and fall.

"Will one plow there with oxen?" You *cannot* run a plow over a
rock.

"For ye have turned judgment into gall, and the fruit of righteousness into hemlock." Israel had done that which was contrary to righteousness. Amos is saying to them, "You've acted foolishly"—as
foolish as I was in riding that old red horse over rocky terrain.

**Ye which rejoice in a thing of nought, which say, Have
we not taken to us horns by our own strength? [Amos
6:13].**

"Have we not taken to us horns by our own strength?" Since in the
Scriptures "horns" are symbolic of power, this is probably a reference
to the military strength of Jeroboam II in which Israel was trusting.

**But, behold I will raise up against you a nation, O house
of Israel, saith the LORD the God of hosts; and they shall
afflict you from the entering in of Hemath unto the river
of the wilderness [Amos 6:14].**

"They shall afflict you from the entering in of Hemath;" that is, from all the way up in Syria, for Hemath was the chief city of Syria.

"Unto the river of the wilderness" should be translated "unto the river of Arabah." Arabah is the river on the other side of the Jordan River which flowed into the Dead Sea.

God is saying, "Through the whole extent of your land this enemy will come down from the north." That enemy was not Ben-hadad of Syria, but it was the king of Assyria who would take these people into captivity.

CHAPTER 7

THEME: Visions of future

Chapter 7 opens the third and last major division of the Book of Amos. These final three chapters contain visions of the future. Although this fellow Amos might be called a clodhopper and a country preacher, he could soar to the heights. Some of the visions the Lord gave to him are quite remarkable.

VISION OF GRASSHOPPERS

Thus hath the Lord GOD shewed unto me; and, behold, he formed grasshoppers in the beginning of the shooting up of the latter growth; and, lo, it was the latter growth after the king's mowings [Amos 7:1].

"Thus hath the Lord GOD shewed unto me; and, behold, he formed grasshoppers in the beginning of the shooting up of the latter growth." These are called grasshoppers in our translation, but they were, of course, locusts.

"And, lo, it was the latter growth after the king's mowings." There were two crops that could be harvested from the land in that day, and the first crop went to the king as taxes. Actually, the people paid more than one-tenth as a tithe. It is estimated that they paid out about three-tenths of what they took from the land, and here we can see an example of that. However, this time, after the king had gotten his due, a plague of grasshoppers or locusts came in and took *their* share so that there was nothing left for the people who had really done the work. This was a judgment that should have shaken the people and should have awakened them.

And it came to pass, that when they had made an end of eating the grass of the land, then I said, O Lord GOD,

forgive, I beseech thee: by whom shall Jacob arise? for
he is small [Amos 7:2].

Amos says to the Lord, "We have been cut down to size. This has so
weakened us that we'll not be able to stand." He calls out to God to
forgive and help them. And notice, the Lord is still patient with
Israel—

The LORD repented for this: It shall not be, saith the LORD
[Amos 7:3].

The Lord said, "I will not do it—I will not weaken you in this way." He
got rid of the grasshoppers, and He gave them a good crop. You would
think that because of His tender mercy the people would return to
God, but they did not.

VISION OF FIRE

Thus hath the Lord GOD shewed unto me: and, behold,
the Lord GOD called to contend by fire, and it devoured
the great deep, and did eat up a part [Amos 7:4].

Many commentators believe the fire here was actually a drought. I am
perfectly willing to say that a drought has to go along with the fire.
When we have dry weather here in Southern California, we often have
fires in the mountains. We have a great many fires here due, in my
judgment, to the carelessness of the public. Many of them have been
started by cigarettes. Nevertheless, the high fire danger is usually
brought on by a drought. But the thing which did the destroying, I
believe, was a literal fire, and I think Amos makes that very clear.

Then said I, O Lord GOD, cease, I beseech thee: by
whom shall Jacob arise? for he is small.

The LORD repented for this: This also shall not be, saith
the Lord GOD [Amos 7:5-6].

Apparently, God sent rain, and the fires were put out. Again, God heard them. When it says that God "repented," it is because of the prayers of the people. God was tenderhearted and would not go through with it. The awful thing, my friend, in rejecting Christ and thus being lost eternally, is the fact that you have to do it against a God who is tenderhearted and who is gracious and loving. God *loves* you, and to sin against that love is an awful, dreadful, and terrible thing.

VISION OF PLUMBLINE

Thus he shewed me: and, behold, the Lord stood upon a wall made by a plumbline, with a plumbline in his hand.

And the Lord said unto me, Amos, what seest thou? And I said, A plumbline. Then said the Lord, Behold, I will set a plumbline in the midst of my people Israel: I will not again pass by them any more [Amos 7:7–8].

We find the plumbline used many places in the Word of God. In Jeremiah 31:38–39 we read, "Behold, the days come, saith the Lord, that the city shall be built to the Lord from the tower of Hananeel unto the gate of the corner. And the measuring line shall yet go forth over against it upon the hill Gareb, and shall compass about to Goath." The "measuring line" is the plumbline, if you please. Every time that you have a vision of the plumbline in Scripture (see Isa. 28:17; Zech. 2:1–2), it means that God is getting ready to judge. In the Book of Daniel, the prophet of God said to King Beshazzar, ". . . Thou art weighed in the balances, and art found wanting" (Dan. 5:27). When God begins to measure either in length or in weight, you can be sure that the people have not measured up to God's requirements, and judgment is the thing which He has in mind. Amos does not intercede for the people again, realizing that God's judgment is just.

And the high places of Isaac shall be desolate, and the sanctuaries of Israel shall be laid waste; and I will rise

**against the house of Jeroboam with the sword [Amos
7:9].**

In other words, God says that Jeroboam will not have peace. God's
principle is, "There is no peace, saith the LORD, unto the wicked" (Isa.
48:22). And Jeroboam will not have peace.

PERSONAL EXPERIENCE OF THE PROPHET

We have wedged in here, between these visions, a little historic interlude, a very personal experience of the prophet Amos. I have considered this section at length in the Introduction, and it also fits very well
into the story here.

> **Then Amaziah the priest of Beth-el sent to Jeroboam
> king of Israel, saying, Amos hath conspired against
> thee in the midst of the house of Israel: the land is not
> able to bear all his words.**
>
> **For thus Amos saith, Jeroboam shall die by the sword,
> and Israel shall surely be led away captive out of their
> own land [Amos 7:10–11].**

If you go back and read verse 9 carefully, you will find that Amaziah is
lying here. This is one of the tragic things that goes on in the church
today. When I teach, I try to speak as simply and as plainly as I possibly
can, and yet I discover that people will misquote me. They represent
me as having said something that I have not said at all. Sometimes this
is done through simply not understanding or failing to comprehend
what was said; other times it is done deliberately.

Amaziah was the priest of the golden calf, and you can imagine the
type of individual he was. He was a hired preacher—he said what the
king wanted him to say. And I suppose that he was very cultured and
used very flowery language. I'm sure he was a good backslapper; he
wasn't a pulpit-pounder but a backslapper. And he could, of course,
entertain. He had charisma, and he was very attractive in many ways.

Amaziah went in and deliberately lied to the king about Amos.

Amos had not said that Jeroboam would perish with the sword, and Jeroboam did not. Amos had said, "And I [God] will rise against the house of Jeroboam with the sword," which meant that warfare would come, and it did come. Israel was finally taken into captivity to Assyria.

> **Also Amaziah said unto Amos, O thou seer, go, flee thee away into the land of Judah, and there eat bread, and prophesy there:**

> **But prophesy not again any more at Beth-el: for it is the king's chapel, and it is the king's court [Amos 7:12-13].**

Amaziah came to Amos, insulted him, and, in effect, called him an ignoramus. I'd like to know where the books are that Amaziah wrote. We have had one book preserved now for over twenty-five hundred years that was written by Amos but none that were written by Amaziah. Amaziah called Amos a country rube and insinuated that he was not fit to speak in the king's chapel. He said, "We want soft words spoken here. We don't want anyone to be offended."

"O thou seer, go, flee thee away into the land of Judah." In other words, "Get out of town and get lost. We don't want you here anymore. You've been speaking in the king's chapel and, after all, you are just not up to it. You're not the caliber of preacher that should be in the pulpit there." Now although Amos was a country man without seminary training, he was no slouch by any means. I hope we agree that he was thoroughly capable of filling the pulpit; in fact, he was a great preacher of God. The people knew when they listened to him that they were getting the Word of God. It is always a comfort to people to have a pastor who is giving the Word of God—that is something very important in these days.

> **Then answered Amos, and said to Amaziah, I was no prophet, neither was I a prophet's son; but I was an herdsman, and a gatherer of sycomore fruit:**

> And the LORD took me as I followed the flock, and the
> LORD said unto me, Go, prophesy unto my people Israel
> [Amos 7:14–15].

Amos answered in such a proper manner that it was evident that he was a moderate man. He wasn't giving out the wild utterances of a prophecy monger. He was no fanatic at all. He said, "Why, I know I'm no prophet. I never claimed to be a prophet. I never went to your seminaries. I'm not even a prophet's son. I was just a herdsman, a gatherer of sycamore fruits, and the Lord told me to prophesy. I'm here because *the Lord* put me here." When a man has that kind of confidence, he's really got confidence, my friend.

A man should be very sure that he has a call from God if he is going to be in the ministry. If there is any doubt in his mind, he ought not to do it. Some say that if you can do anything else, then don't go into the ministry. I don't quite agree with that because a great many of us could have done something else and might have preferred doing it, by the way. The important thing is: Did God call you? If God has called you, my friend, you ought not to let anything stand in the way.

Now Amos has a personal prophesy for Amaziah, and this is strong medicine for him. Many folk say to me, "Dr. McGee, you are very harsh at times with certain groups or certain churches." In answer to that, I can truly say that I carry no bias or hatred in my heart against any of those that I mention. What I am trying to do is to be sweet and nice, and I ought not to speak harshly. Love is to be the theme today: Love, love, love! My friend, listen to Amos as he talks to "brother Amaziah"—

> Now therefore hear thou the word of the LORD: Thou sayest, Prophesy not against Israel, and drop not thy word against the house of Isaac.

> Therefore thus saith the LORD; Thy wife shall be an harlot in the city, and thy sons and thy daughters shall fall by the sword, and thy land shall be divided by line; and thou shalt die in a polluted land: and Israel shall surely go into captivity forth of his land [Amos 7:16–17].

"Therefore thus saith the LORD"—Amos says that he has a word from God to this man Amaziah. This is a very disturbing prophecy, and it's a very strong prophecy, but the thing is that it was a *true* prophecy. When Assyria came down, they did make the women harlots. The sons and daughters were destroyed, and those who were not destroyed were taken into captivity. And this old priest of the golden calf, Amaziah, was taken into Assyrian captivity. I am sure that Amaziah's word on his deathbed would have been like that of old cardinal Wolsey (whom I mentioned earlier) who wished that he had served his God as he had served his king. Cardinal Wolsey had tried to play politics with Henry VIII and did not really tell him what the Word of God had to say.

If we as ministers fail to give out the Word of God, there is no reason for us to point our fingers at the politicians in Washington and accuse them of failing our country and jeopardizing our nation. My friend in the ministry, if you are not giving out the Word of God, there is no other traitor in this land today as guilty as you are. If you are called to be a minister, you are called to be a minister of *the Word of God*. If you are not giving that Word out, you are a traitor to the cause of Christ today. Those are strong words, I know, just as Amos' words were strong.

CHAPTER 8

THEME: Vision of basket of summer fruit

This is the fourth vision, and it takes in the entire eighth chapter of this book. It is important to get the meaning of this vision because that will help us in the interpretation of passages that come later on. Especially it will clarify some of the things that our Lord Jesus said.

Thus hath the Lord God shewed unto me: and behold a basket of summer fruit [Amos 8:1].

A great deal can be said about a basket of summer fruit. I love fruit. To me all fruits are delicious. I enjoy the citrus fruits of California or Florida, the fruits of northern California and Oregon and Washington. Wherever I am, I enjoy the fruit produced in that locality. There is nothing more attractive than a basket of summer fruit, and that basket of summer fruit has a message.

First of all, a basket of summer fruit represents a harvest. It tells us that the tree is no longer producing. My apricot tree had some lovely apricots on it this past summer, but there is no need for me to go out now to see if there is fruit on the tree. The limbs are bare; there is no fruit. The harvest is past. There will be no fruit until next year. So we see that although a basket of summer fruit is delightful and delicious, it also speaks of the end of the harvest.

A basket of summer fruit also tells us of rapid spoilage and quick deterioration. Back in the time of World War II, a missionary from South America wrote to us from the East that she was coming to the West Coast. Since she was a personal friend and would be staying with us during her time in California, she told us the day of her arrival. You may remember that in those days trains were crowded and the military had priority over all else. When our friend reached Chicago, she learned that her reservation had been cancelled. She had to wait a week before she could come out to California. We had prepared the guest room for her for the day we had expected her to arrive. I had gone out and picked some lovely apricots off my tree and had put a basket of apricots in her room. When we got the telegram from her telling us of her delay, we just closed the door to her room. We forgot all about the basket of apricots. Then when the time came for her to arrive, we opened the door to her room, and I want to tell you the odor was not very pleasant! In fact, it took us weeks to get the odor out of that room. There is a message in a basket of summer fruit. God gives us a dramatic and a figurative illustration.

> **And he said, Amos, what seest thou? And I said, A basket of summer fruit. Then said the LORD unto me, The end is come upon my people of Israel; I will not again pass by them any more [Amos 8:2].**

We have seen in chapter 7 in the previous visitations of God's judgments that Amos prayed for the survival of Israel and that God changed His mind and withheld His hand. But now the basket of summer fruit indicates that the harvest is past. The jig is up. The northern kingdom of Israel has come to the end of the line. Judgment will come, and harvest is symbolic of that.

Since harvest speaks of a time of judgment and falls at the end of an age, I think that some things our Lord said are misunderstood if one does not understand what is meant by ". . . The harvest truly is plenteous, but the labourers are few; Pray ye therefore the Lord of the harvest, that he will send forth labourers into his harvest" (Matt. 9:37–38). Our Lord was speaking at the end of an age when the dispensation of the law was coming to an end. Christ was going to go to the cross. He said that He needed harvesters to go out into Israel.

After His death on the cross, it is a different picture. For this age of grace He gives His parable of the sower. A sower went forth to sow seed. ". . . Go ye into all the world, and preach the gospel . . ." (Mark 16:15), is the message for our age. Go out into the world and sow the seed. This is the time for sowing the Word of God. My business and your business is just sowing the seed. It is the Lord's business to do the converting. We believe that the Spirit of God will take the Word of God and make a son of God. We are just seedsowers. We are not harvesters. Harvest speaks of judgment, and it speaks of the end of an age. Our business today is to be out sowing the seed. I wish so much that I could get this message across to people. I wish I could motivate all believers to do what God has called us to do. Our business is to sow the seed of the Word of God.

> **And the songs of the temple shall be howlings in that day, saith the Lord God: there shall be many dead bodies in every place; they shall cast them forth with silence [Amos 8:3].**

The place for praising God will be changed into a place of waiting. The place of rejoicing before God will be changed into a place of weeping. The slain bodies will be everywhere. This is a terrifying prophecy.

> **Hear this, O ye that swallow up the needy, even to make the poor of the land to fail [Amos 8:4].**

Again God is speaking of the exploitation of the poor. Although I have commented on this before, I feel it is important for us to realize how God feels about the poor of this world. I have experienced being poor. My dad was a workman. I remember him wearing his overalls and drawing his paycheck on Saturday. After he would pay the grocery bill and the doctor bill and the rent, he always gave my sister and me a nickel each, but I remember one Saturday night when he had only one nickel left. He told me to go to the store and buy a sack of candy. I got gumdrops because I could get a big sack of them for a nickel in those days, and my sister and I divided the gumdrops.

My dad died when I was fourteen, and it was up to me to support my mother and sister. At fourteen I had to secure a special permit to get a job. Then, after I was converted and felt called to the ministry, some folk took an interest in me and helped me get through school. Believe me, I am for the poverty program—but not the one we have had in our society that puts money in the pockets of those who already have it. I want to see a poverty program that will really help the poor get on their feet and enable them to work.

In the days of Amos, God accuses them of even making "the poor of the land to fail." That is, the poor were brought down to such a low poverty level that they never could escape from it. The poor always suffer more acutely in a godless nation—I don't think that statement can be successfully contradicted.

> **Saying, When will the new moon be gone, that we may sell corn? and the sabbath, that we may set forth wheat, making the ephah small, and the shekel great, and falsifying the balances by deceit? [Amos 8:5].**

If you had been among the people in that day—especially down in Jerusalem at the temple—you would have wondered what the Lord was talking about. You would have seen them going through the rituals which God had prescribed. But, you see, God knew what was in their hearts. "The new moon" and "the sabbath" were holy days on which business was not transacted. God is saying that even when the rich went to the temple to praise God, they were so greedy and covetous that they were thinking about business the next day and how they could make more money by cheating their customers. They not only practiced their sin during the week, but they carried it into the temple. What a picture this gives us of Israel in that day—and of modern man as well.

> **That we may buy the poor for silver, and the needy for a pair of shoes; yea, and sell the refuse of the wheat? [Amos 8:6].**

"That we may buy the poor for silver." The poor even had to sell themselves into slavery. That was permitted in that land under the Mosaic system. They would buy the needy for a pair of shoes—that's how cheap they were! And they would sell the poor the refuse of the wheat. That means they got the "seconds," the leftovers which an honest dealer throws away.

I have never felt right about giving old clothes to help the poor in the church. I have never felt they should be given the leftovers of anything. When I was just starting my ministry, a dairyman in Georgia told me he generally had a quart of skim milk left over and he would leave it for me since I preached in a little church there. I didn't accept the milk even though I could have used it. I felt it would not be fair to the man to give him the feeling he was doing a great service to the Lord by giving his leftovers. Remember how David said, ". . . neither will I offer burnt offerings unto the LORD my God of that which doth cost me nothing . . ." (2 Sam. 24:24).

It is no accident that the Lord Jesus, when He was here on earth, sat and watched how the people gave in the temple. Was that His business? Yes. And He is interested in how much *we* give to Him and how much we keep for ourselves.

I guess you can tell that I can identify with Amos. Maybe the reason I love this man Amos so much is that he talks my language. He was a poor man himself, and he says the thing that I understand.

You see, Amos is explaining why Israel was like a basket of summer fruit. The goodness of Israel was just as perishable and just as soon deteriorated as summer fruit. One evidence of this was the way they treated the poor.

The LORD hath sworn by the excellency of Jacob, Surely I will never forget any of their works [Amos 8:7].

"The LORD hath sworn by the excellency of Jacob." The excellency of Jacob is the Lord Jesus Christ. The Lord has sworn by the Messiah who is coming. No oath could be taken that is higher than that.

Now notice what it is that He has sworn: "Surely I will never forget any of their works." As we have seen previously in this book, God does not forget the works of any of us—believer or unbeliever. Those of us who are believers will one day ". . . appear before the judgment seat of Christ; that every one may receive the things done in his body, according to that he hath done, whether it be good or bad" (2 Cor. 5:10). In the days of Amos, they had heaped up sins unto the day of God's wrath, and He remembered every one of them.

Shall not the land tremble for this, and every one mourn that dwelleth therein? and it shall rise up wholly as a flood; and it shall be cast out and drowned, as by the flood of Egypt [Amos. 8:8].

Some commentators think this refers to an earthquake. That is possible, and I certainly wouldn't want to rule that out. However, I think it is the fact that God is coming down hard upon them in judgment that makes the land tremble. Even today one cannot go through places like Samaria and the rugged hill country around Gilgal and Beth-el without being impressed by the frightful state of the land. It once was a very fruitful area with a great deal of vegetation, including a great many trees, but today the land has been pretty much denuded. It shows the evidence of judgment upon it. God came down heavily upon the land. We will see in the next chapter that the promise for the future includes a promise for the land.

When we study prophecy, we need to remember that whether God promised judgment or blessing, the land was involved as well as the people. That is one reason why I cannot accept the idea that the prophecies of the Scripture are being fulfilled in the present return of Jews to that land. Although they have returned physically to the land, they have not returned spiritually to the Lord. It is obvious today that God's blessing is not upon that land. It hasn't changed. It is true that a great deal of hard work has gone into it; areas have been recovered from swamps, and irrigation has reached the desert in many places (which has made it blossom like a rose), but those places are few and far between even in that small land. Therefore, it cannot be said that these great prophecies are being fulfilled. Israel's last return to the land has not yet taken place. Let's remember that there are more Jews in New York City than there are in the entire nation of Israel—that ought to tell us something.

And it shall come to pass in that day, saith the Lord God, that I will cause the sun to go down at noon, and I will darken the earth in the clear day [Amos 8:9].

Now here is Amos speaking of "that day," which we have already seen is a technical expression that refers to the day of the Lord. And generally it refers to the Great Tribulation because that comes first—the day begins at night as far as Israel was concerned.

Amos gives a mingling of prophecy of the near future and the far distant future. The Day of the Lord has not yet arrived. The sun has not gone down at noon, nor has the earth been darkened in the clear day. When Amos wrote this, this was still in the far distant future.

Now he turns to the more immediate future for Israel—

> **And I will turn your feasts into mourning, and all your songs into lamentation; and I will bring up sackcloth upon all loins, and baldness upon every head; and I will make it as the mourning of an only son, and the end thereof as a bitter day [Amos 8:10].**

"And I will turn your feasts into mourning." God gave to the nation Israel seven feasts. The males of Israel were required to come before Him for three of those great feasts. They were to come with rejoicing. It was to be a time of praise and thanksgiving and glorifying God. Now God says that since they have been celebrating the feasts but not giving praise to Him, He will turn their feasts into mourning. They will become the very opposite of what He intended them to be, ". . . and all your songs into lamentation." When God's judgment falls upon them, there will be no more singing—no more joy—only lamentation.

Although I am certainly no music critic, I have been interested to observe the trend of modern music. When I was a young fellow, the popular music was the blues. That was followed by jazz and then rock and roll. Today it is hard rock. Do you detect any joy in that music? Oh, the songs have a beat to them so that you hop up and down like a yo-yo, but it is almost a mindless kind of motion which requires no thinking. That kind of music stimulates the flesh but certainly gives no real joy. This is the type of music that the world produces. It is mournful and it is tragic. When I had the privilege of being in Vienna, I attended an opera there. It was the first opera I had ever heard, and I

have to confess that I enjoyed it. However, it was a tragedy. The boy
didn't get the girl. It was a tragic story, and the songs were lamenta-
tions and wailings. Now that is the type of music which the world
produces. I am struck with the fact that God has said, "I will
turn . . .all your songs into lamentation."

"And I will make it as the mourning of an only son, and the end
thereof as a bitter day." Sackcloth on all loins and baldness on every
head are indications of the deepest mourning. This was literally fulfilled in the judgment that was to come unto them presently.

**Behold, the days come, saith the Lord GOD, that I will
send a famine in the land, not a famine of bread, nor a
thirst for water, but of hearing the words of the LORD
[Amos 8:11].**

Here is a most unusual famine. God had given them His Word, and
they had rejected it. They had despised it and turned aside from it.
Now God tells that the day is coming when they will no longer have the
privilege of hearing His Word.

God tells any church or any nation that if they will not hear His
Word after He has given it to them, He will withdraw it from them. I
think we can see this happening in America. There has been a rejection of the Word of God. The churches have turned to liberalism, and
the Word of God is no longer preached. There has come a famine of the
Word of God. So many of the formerly great churches of this country,
the great downtown churches, have turned from the Word of God. As a
consequence, many of them have had to close shop. Others are just
barely operating, and many of them are operating in the red. Even
those which have stayed open have lost their influence and have lost
their drawing power.

Actually, very little of the Word of God is getting out in this land
today. There is a Gideon Bible in every room in every hotel and motel in
this country. Nearly everyone *owns* a Bible. But who is studying it?
Who is reading it? Who is believing it? I think we are beginning to see
the famine of the Word of God in this country.

**And they shall wander from sea to sea, and from the
north even to the east, they shall run to and fro to seek
the word of the LORD, and shall not find it [Amos 8:12].**

The distraught people will wander from sea to sea seeking the Word of
God but will not find it. God in His great love for His chosen people
had sent His Word by prophet after prophet, but they had rejected His
Word, persecuted and even slain His prophets. Now one of God's judgments will be His silence.

We see something of this same situation in our own land. I receive
numerous letters from folk all over the country who tell me that they
have no Bible teaching in their town or community and haven't had
any for many years. The famine has already set in for this land of ours.
My friend, the most important thing in the world that we can do is to
give out God's Word by every means at our disposal.

**In that day shall the fair virgins and young men faint for
thirst [Amos 8:13].**

Even the young people, the most hopeful and vigorous members of
society, will faint for thirst after the Word of God.

**They that swear by the sin of Samaria, and say, Thy god,
O Dan, liveth; and, The manner of Beer-sheba liveth;
even they shall fall, and never rise up again [Amos
8:14].**

It was their custom to swear in the name of their gods. "The sin of
Samaria" refers to the golden calf which was located at Beth-el. The
second golden calf was located at Dan, and there was an idolatrous
sanctuary at Beersheba, as we have seen. God's judgment upon them
from such idolatry concludes this chapter: "they shall fall, and never
rise up again." This indicates the dissolution and permanent downfall
of the northern kingdom. The ten tribes are going into captivity, and
they will never return as the northern kingdom of Israel. When they
come back to their land, they will come as part of the twelve tribes.

CHAPTER 9

THEME: *Vision of worldwide dispersion, regathering and restoration*

This chapter concludes the message of judgment which Amos has been delivering to Israel. Then Amos looks into the far future and gives the glorious prospect of the restored kingdom of Israel.

> **I saw the Lord standing upon the altar: and he said, Smite the lintel of the door, that the posts may shake: and cut them in the head, all of them; and I will slay the last of them with the sword: he that fleeth of them shall not flee away, and he that escapeth of them shall not be delivered [Amos 9:1].**

This describes the coming of the Assyrians. We need to understand that "the altar" is not the altar of Solomon's temple in Jerusalem but is probably the altar of the temple to Baal in Samaria. I have seen the ruins of this temple in Samaria.

"Smite the lintel of the door, that the posts may shake: and cut them in the head, all of them." At the time of the siege, the people would seek refuge in the temples, but the temples would be brought down so suddenly that many of the people would be trapped when the pillars crumbled.

"He that fleeth of them shall not flee away, and he that escapeth of them shall not be delivered." Those who would escape alive from the city would be carried into captivity.

Now notice this frightful statement—

> **Though they dig into hell, thence shall mine hand take them; though they climb up to heaven, thence will I bring them down [Amos 9:2].**

"Though they dig into hell." The word translated "hell" is the Hebrew word *sheol*, meaning "the grave or the place of the dead."

There are two things which cause the terror of the wicked. In our day, folk have been so brainwashed by our society that many of them try to blot it out of their minds; but if they give any thought to it at all, the two things which bring terror to the heart of the wicked person are the omnipresence and the immutability of God. God is omnipresent; that is, He is everywhere. Even death cannot separate you from Him. And the immutability of God means that God never changes. Jesus Christ is the same yesterday, today, and forever. These two truths are a great comfort to God's children, but they are frightening to the wicked.

To the child of God the omnipresence of God assures him that God will never leave him. The Lord Jesus said, ". . . I will never leave thee, nor forsake thee" (Heb. 13:5). How wonderful that is! Also He said, ". . . him that cometh to me I will in no wise cast out" (John 6:37). When He receives you, He receives you for eternity. No one can take you out of His hand; and, if you are in His hand, you are very close to Him, you see. The Lord Jesus also likened our relationship to Him to that of a vine and its branches. What can be closer to a vine than its branch? The omnipresence of God is a great comfort to the believer.

However, for the unbeliever, the omnipresence of God is a terror. Many people commit suicide because they want to get away from it all. A prominent man here in Southern California left a suicide note which read, "I want to end it all and get rid of this life." Well, he got rid of his problems and a great many things which were annoying him here—he was in deep trouble—but he didn't get rid of God. Death didn't separate him from God. David understood this when he wrote, "Whither shall I go from thy spirit? or whither shall I flee from thy presence? If I ascend up into heaven, thou art there: if I make my bed in hell, behold, thou art there" (Ps. 139:7-8). And the poet Francis Thompson was not being irreverent when he characterized God as "the hound of heaven" because, regardless of who you are, God is right on your track. You cannot get rid of Him.

Then there is the immutability of God. God didn't learn anything new by reading the morning newspaper. The president or the Senate or the college professors or the scientists cannot teach God anything that is new to Him. He doesn't change His mind. He never changes. "Jesus Christ the same yesterday, and to-day, and for ever" (Heb. 13:8). That is wonderful for the child of God to know. The same One who walked by the Sea of Galilee, who was so gracious and merciful to people, is still the same One who walks with the believer today.

> **And though they hide themselves in the top of Carmel, I will search and take them out thence; and though they be hid from my sight in the bottom of the sea, thence will I command the serpent, and he shall bite them [Amos 9:3].**

"And though they hide themselves in the top of Carmel, I will search and take them out thence." The city of Haifa is located on Carmel today. Mount Carmel is wooded and rises to a height of about eighteen hundred feet. I have been there several times and have noted the caves which are along the sides of that mountain. It is said that there are over a thousand caves there, especially on the side toward the sea. But even there God said he would search them out. And although they should try to hide in the bottom of the sea, they would find God there. They could not escape Him.

> **And though they go into captivity before their enemies, thence will I command the sword, and it shall slay them: and I will set mine eyes upon them for evil, and not for good [Amos 9:4].**

"And though they go into captivity before their enemies"—that is, going voluntarily in order to spare their lives, they still will not escape God's judgment.

My friend, the wicked do well to fear God and to fear the future. There is no escape for them. The man who commits suicide, thinking that he will get rid of his troubles, will move into real trouble when he faces God. It is like jumping from the frying pan into the fire—and *that* almost literally.

> And the Lord GOD of hosts is he that toucheth the land,
> and it shall melt, and all that dwell therein shall mourn:
> and it shall rise up wholly like a flood; and shall be
> drowned, as by the flood of Egypt [Amos 9:5].

You cannot go through that land today without being conscious of the fact that it certainly is no longer a land of milk and honey. Even with all the irrigation and cultivation, it is far from that. Judgment has come upon it.

When I was in a hotel there, I met a lovely Jewish couple in the elevator. We began to talk about the land. They had come out to buy an apartment. They thought they might retire permanently to Israel or at least spend part of the year there. He told me very candidly, "Although we bought the apartment because we want to help our people in this land, we really don't ever expect to use it. I don't think this is the land that the Bible says it is." Obviously, he had not read the prophecy of Amos and did not realize that God's judgment had come upon the land.

> It is he that buildeth his stories in the heaven, and hath
> founded his troop in the earth; he that calleth for the
> waters of the sea, and poureth them out upon the face of
> the earth: the LORD is his name [Amos 9:6].

In this beautiful way Amos is reminding his people of the omnipotence of God. Not only is He omnipresent, but He is also omnipotent. It is He who does all of this. Out yonder in the heavens, the sun, the moon, the planets, the tremendous galaxies, the quasars, the whole universe obeys God. He has made certain laws by which they are to move, and they obey those laws. But little man—little man is in rebellion against the omnipotent God. In effect, Amos is asking Israel, "Do you think we can escape such a God?"

Now here is one of the strangest statements in the Bible, and it is quite wonderful—

> Are ye not as children of the Ethiopians unto me, O chil-
> dren of Israel? saith the LORD. Have not I brought up Is-

rael out of the land of Egypt? and the Philistines from
Caphtor, and the Syrians from Kir? [Amos 9:7].

When God wanted them to know how much He loved them, He said, "I
love you as I love the Ethiopians!" At the time that the Italians under
Mussolini invaded Ethiopia in 1935, I made a study of the biblical
prophecies concerning Ethiopia. It was amazing to me to discover the
place which Ethiopia has in the program of God for the future. It is a
nation which may seem very unimportant to us, but it is very important to God.

> Behold, the eyes of the Lord GOD are upon the sinful
> kingdom, and I will destroy it from off the face of the
> earth; saving that I will not utterly destroy the house of
> Jacob, saith the LORD [Amos 9:8].

"The sinful kingdom" is Israel, of course. "I will destroy it from off the
face of the earth" means that He will destroy it as a separate kingdom.
When God returns the people of Israel to their land, they will not be a
divided kingdom but will be one nation under the sovereignty of the
One sitting on the throne of David.

> For, lo, I will command, and I will sift the house of Is-
> rael among all nations, like as corn is sifted in a sieve,
> yet shall not the least grain fall upon the earth [Amos
> 9:9].

"I will sift the house of Israel among all nations." If you want to know
where the so called "lost tribes of Israel" are, look in your phone book
for the Cothens, the Goldbergs, etc. They are scattered throughout the
world, but they are not "lost" as far as God is concerned. "Yet shall not
the least grain fall upon the earth." God will not lose one of them.

> All the sinners of my people shall die by the sword,
> which say, The evil shall not overtake nor prevent us
> [Amos 9:10].

How about the sinners? They are going to die. He will judge the individuals who won't turn to Him. We have the same analogy in the contemporary church. Not all church members are saved. Believe me, if you have been a pastor as long as I have, you would *know* that not all church members are genuine believers—but they *are* church members. And the apostle Paul says, ". . . For they are not all Israel, which are of Israel" (Rom. 9:6). There are two kinds of Israelites, the natural and the spiritual Israel. Although "not the least grain" will fall to the ground, all sinners of the nation will perish, especially the defiant ones whom Amos has been addressing.

This brings us to the final vision of Amos, that of the worldwide regathering and restoration of the kingdom of the Lord. Amos saw beyond the terrible days of judgment and scattering of His people, even beyond the Great Tribulation (which is still future in our day).

In that day will I raise up the tabernacle of David that is fallen, and close up the breaches thereof; and I will raise up his ruins, and I will build it as in the days of old [Amos 9:11].

The phrase "in that day" refers to the last days of Israel. "In that day will I raise up the tabernacle of David that is fallen." To follow through on this, listen to James in Acts 15 where he quotes this prophecy of Amos: "And after they had held their peace, James answered, saying, Men and brethren, hearken unto me: Simeon hath declared how God at the first did visit the Gentiles, to take out of them a people for his name. And to this agree the words of the prophets; as it is written, After this I will return, and will build again the tabernacle of David, which is fallen down; and I will build again the ruins thereof, and I will set it up: That the residue of men might seek after the Lord, and all the Gentiles, upon whom my name is called, saith the Lord, who doeth all these things. Known unto God are all his works from the beginning of the world" (Acts 15:13–18).

Today God is calling out a people for His name among the Gentiles. After this He will raise up the tabernacle of David. In other words, God is speaking of the kingdom age, the Millennium, the greatest day which is yet in the future.

> That they may possess the remnant of Edom, and of all the heathen, which are called by my name, saith the LORD that doeth this [Amos 9:12].

There will be many nations which will enter the Millennium.

> Behold, the days come, saith the LORD, that the plowman shall overtake the reaper, and the treader of grapes him that soweth seed; and the mountains shall drop sweet wine, and all the hills shall melt [Amos 9:13].

This is the proof of what I have mentioned previously, that when the people of Israel are being blessed, the land of Israel is being blessed. The people and the land belong together. God makes it clear that when *He* returns the people of Israel to their land, it will again be the land of milk and honey. The land is not that now; so I take it that the present return is not the one which is predicted. Although Jews are returning to their land, they are not returning to their God.

> And I will bring again the captivity of my people of Israel, and they shall build the waste cities, and inhabit them; and they shall plant vineyards, and drink the wine thereof; they shall also make gardens, and eat the fruit of them [Amos 9:14].

God is going to restore Israel to the land. Never again will it be the southern kingdom of Judah and the northern kingdom of Israel. It will all be Israel, an undivided kingdom, as it was in the beginning of its history. It will be all twelve tribes. They are scattered over the whole world today. They are sifted among all nations. Any idea that "the lost tribes" are the people of Great Britain and of the United States is unscriptural. The prophecy clearly states that they will be sifted among all nations. Just look around you. Has God done that, or hasn't He done it? But it will not be that way forever. God will return them to the land. "I will bring again the captivity of my people of Israel, and they shall build the waste cities, and inhabit them."

And I will plant them upon their land, and they shall no more be pulled up out of their land which I have given them, saith the LORD thy God [Amos 9:15].

When God puts them in the land, they will be there permanently.

These are the things God has said He will do for His people: (1) He is going to restore the Davidic dynasty. Who do you think will be the king? It will be a son of David by the name of Jesus, born in Bethlehem of the houses and lineage of David. He will be the ruler. (2) Israel will take her place among the nations of the world. She will no longer go to the United Nations with her hat in her hand (nor will she be shutting out Arabs). She will be a nation that is going to be blessed of God and will occupy a place among the nations of the world. (3) In addition to this, there will be a conversion of the nations of the world! This will occur after the church leaves this earth. The greatest conversion to Christ is still in the future. What a day that will be! When God returns Israel to her land, (4) they will build the waste cities and inhabit them. (5) They will eat the fruit of their gardens and drink the wine of their vineyards. The curse on the land will be lifted, and it will produce bountifully. (6) And the people of Israel "shall no more be pulled up out of their land which I have given them, saith the LORD thy God."

BIBLIOGRAPHY
(Recommended for Further Study)

Cohen, Gary G. and Vandervey, H. Ronald. *Hosea and Amos*. Chicago, Illinois: Moody Press, 1981.

Feinberg, Charles L. *The Minor Prophets*. Chicago, Illinois: Moody Press, 1976.

Gaebelein, Arno C. *The Annotated Bible*. 1917. Reprint. Neptune, New Jersey: Loizeaux Brothers, 1971.

Ironside, H. A. *The Minor Prophets*. Neptune, New Jersey: Loizeaux Brothers, n.d.

Jensen, Irving L. *Minor Prophets of Israel*. Chicago, Illinois: Moody Press, 1975.

Tatford, Fredrick A. *The Minor Prophets*. Minneapolis, Minnesota: Klock & Klock, n.d.

Unger, Merrill F. *Unger's Commentary on the Old Testament*, Vol. 2. Chicago, Illinois: Moody Press, 1982.

OBADIAH

The Book of

OBADIAH

INTRODUCTION

The name *Obadiah* means "servant of Jehovah." He is one of four prophets about whom we know absolutely nothing except that he wrote prophecy. The other three prophets are Habakkuk, Haggai, and Malachi. These four prophets are cloaked in anonymity. Obadiah is like a ghost writer in that he is there, but we do not know him. He lived up to his name, for he was a servant of Jehovah. A servant boasts of no genealogy neither exploits nor experiences. He doesn't push himself forward. He has to demonstrate by what he *does* that he can even claim the place of a servant. So Obadiah is just a prophet who wrote one of the great prophecies of the Scripture. Dr. Pusey said, "God has willed that his name alone and this brief prophecy should be known to the world." Obadiah is a little book, but it is an example of an atomic bomb in the Bible. It is a small thing, but it has a potent message.

The chief difficulty with the prophecy of Obadiah is where to fit it into the history of the nation Israel. There are some who give the date of 887 B.C., which fixes the time during the reign of Jehoram and the bloody Athaliah (see 2 Kings 8:16–26). Dr. Pusey placed it during the reign of Jehoshaphat (see 2 Chron. 17:7). Although the name *Obadiah* does occur in this passage, it was a common name in that day and probably was not the same Obadiah who wrote this prophecy. Canon Farrar gave the date as 587 B.C., and Dr. Moorehead concurred in this, suggesting that Obadiah was probably a contemporary of Jeremiah's. The whole question seems to hinge on verse 11: "In the day that thou stoodest on the other side, in the day that the strangers carried away captive his forces, and foreigners entered into his gates, and cast lots upon Jerusalem, even thou wast as one of them." Either this was written as prophecy before it happened, or it is an historical record of what did happen. The natural interpretation, of course, is to accept it as history rather than prophecy, which places the date of Obadiah's prophecy around 587 B.C., after the Babylonian captivity and during the ministry of the prophet Jeremiah.

The little kingdom of Edom is the subject of this brief prophecy. Verse 6 is the key verse: "How are the things of Esau searched out! how are his hidden things sought up!"

OUTLINE

I. **Edom—Destruction, vv. 1–16**
   A. Charge against Edom, vv. 1–9
   B. Crime of Edom, vv. 10–14
   C. Catastrophe to Edom, vv. 15–16
      (Poetic justice [lex talionis]—law of retaliation)

II. **Israel—Restoration, vv. 17–21**
   A. Condition of Israel, v. 17
   B. Conflagration of the House of Esau, v. 18
   C. Consummation of All Things, vv. 19–21
      ("And the kingdom shall be the Lord's")

OBADIAH

THEME: Edom—destruction; and Israel—restoration

Obadiah is the shortest book in the Old Testament—only twenty-one verses. There are many folk who feel that this book is not worth reading and that if it were omitted from the Bible, it would not be missed. However, the brevity of the message does not render it less important or less significant. Like the other Minor Prophets, the message is primary, it is pertinent, it is practical, and it is poignant. It is a message that can be geared into this day in which we are living.

None of these so-called Minor Prophets are extinct volcanoes; rather, they are distinct action. There is no cold ash in any of them; they are spewing hot lava. Obadiah's prophecy is of devastating judgment against the little kingdom of Edom.

CHARGE AGAINST EDOM

The vision of Obadiah. Thus saith the Lord GOD concerning Edom; We have heard a rumor from the LORD, and an ambassador is sent among the heathen, Arise ye, and let us rise up against her in battle [Obad. 1].

Obadiah tells us immediately, bluntly, and to the point that this is a vision given to him by God Himself.

Who is Obadiah? As I mentioned in the Introduction, he is one of the Minor Prophets about whom we know absolutely nothing. His name was a very common one in Israel, and it means "servant of Jehovah."

"Thus saith the Lord GOD concerning Edom." Edom is the key to this little book, and so we shall have to go back to Genesis to determine the identity of Edom. In Genesis, where we have the record of the generations of Esau, notice this comment: "Now these are the generations of Esau, who is Edom" (Gen. 36:1). Also this: "Thus dwelt Esau in mount Seir: Esau is Edom. And these are the generations of Esau the father of the Edomites in mount Seir" (Gen. 36:8–9).

That is the record that is given to us here, and it is repeated three times. Although I am sure Moses did not know, the Spirit of God knew that this would need to be emphasized—Esau is Edom and Edom is Esau. The Edomites were those who were descended from Esau, just as the Israelites are those who are descended from Jacob.

The story of Esau is that of twin brothers, sons of Isaac and Rebekah. The boys were not identical twins; actually, they were opposites. The record given back in Genesis 25 begins as Rebekah is about to give birth to these twins: "And the children struggled together within her; and she said, If it be so, why am I thus? And she went to inquire of the LORD. And the LORD said unto her, Two nations are in thy womb, and two manner of people shall be separated from thy bowels; and the one people shall be stronger than the other people; and the elder shall serve the younger" (Gen. 25:22–23). From the very beginning these two brothers were struggling against each other. Esau was an outdoor fellow who loved to hunt. Jacob would rather stay in the house and learn to cook. He was tied to his mama's apron strings. However, Jacob had a spiritual discernment that Esau did not have. Esau was a man of the flesh and did not care for spiritual things. In fact, he so discounted his birthright that he traded it to Jacob for a bowl of soup! "And Esau said to Jacob, Feed me, I pray thee, with that same red pottage; for I am faint: therefore was his name called Edom. And Jacob said, Sell me this day thy birthright. And Esau said, Behold, I am at the point to die: and what profit shall this birthright do to me? And Jacob said, Swear to me this day; and he sware unto him: and he sold his birthright unto Jacob. Then Jacob gave Esau bread and pottage of lentiles; and he did eat and drink, and rose up, and went his way: thus Esau despised his birthright" (Gen. 25:30–34).

He didn't sell his birthright because he was so hungry that he was about to perish, nor because there wasn't anything else to eat in the home of Isaac, but because his was a desire of the flesh and he was willing to trade all of his spiritual heritage for a whim of the moment. The man who had the birthright was in contact with God, and he was the priest of his family. He was the man who had a covenant from God.

He was the man who had a relationship with God. In effect Esau said, "I would rather have a bowl of soup than have a relationship with God."

This is an illustration of a great truth for believers today. It is a picture of Christians. A believer has two natures within him, and they are struggling with each other and against each other. In Galatians 5:17 Paul says, "For the flesh lusteth [wars] against the Spirit, and the Spirit against the flesh: and these are contrary the one to the other: so that ye cannot do the things that ye would." These are the two natures of the believer, the new nature and the old nature. They are opposed to each other. Esau pictures the flesh, the old nature, and Jacob pictures the spirit, the new nature.

The name *Edom* means "red or sunburned." A sunburn occurs when the skin is able to absorb the rays of light except the rays that make it red. The sunburned man in Scripture is the man who could not absorb the light of heaven, and it burned him. My friend, the light of heaven will either save you or burn you. You will either absorb it, or you will be burned by it. This is always true. Esau represented the flesh. He became Edom. Jacob, who became Israel, a prince with God, represents the spirit.

Having seen Esau in the first book of the Old Testament, look now at the last book of the Old Testament and read this strange language: "I have loved you, saith the LORD. Yet ye say, Wherein hast thou loved us? Was not Esau Jacob's brother? saith the LORD: yet I loved Jacob, And I hated Esau . . ." (Mal. 1:2-3). This is a strange thing for God to say—"I loved Jacob, and I hated Esau." It immediately presents a problem.

A student once approached Dr. Griffith Thomas with this question, "Dr. Thomas, I am having a problem with this statement in Malachi. I cannot understand why God says He hated Esau." Dr. Thomas replied, "Young man, I am having a problem with that verse also, but my problem is different from yours. I can understand why He hated Esau, but I cannot understand why He loved Jacob."

Well, the thing that lends importance to the little Book of Obadiah is that it is the only place in the Word of God where we find the explanation of why God hated Esau.

Ginsburg, the great Hebrew Scholar, translated Obadiah 6 like this:

"How are the things of Esau stripped bare!" In other words, they are laid out in the open for you to look at for the first time. Obadiah puts the microscope down on Esau, and when you look through the eyepiece you see *Edom*. Not only did Obadiah focus the microscope on him, but Obadiah *is* God's microscope! Come here and look through the microscope. Look! One Esau—oh, he is magnified!—one Esau is now 250,000 little Esaus, and that is Edom. The photographer takes a miniature and makes a great enlarged picture. He says, "I blew up the picture." Obadiah is the "blown up" picture of Esau. You inflate a tire tube to find a tiny leak in it. Just so, Obadiah presents Esau inflated so that you can see where the flaw is in his life, and you can see why God said He hated him. What at the beginning was a little pimple under the skin is now a raging and angry cancer. What was small in Esau is now magnified 100,000 times in the nation. God did not say at the beginning that He hated Esau; He had to wait until he became a nation and revealed the thing that caused God to hate him.

God never said that He hated Esau or loved Jacob until He came to the last book in the Old Testament. Both men have become nations, Edom and Israel. Israel has been mightily used of God through the centuries. Israel produced men like Moses, Joshua, Samuel, David, Hezekiah, Nehemiah, Ezra, and on down the line. But the nation that came from Esau became a godless nation. Edom turned its back upon God, and what was it that caused God to hate Esau and to hate the nation?

> **Behold, I have made thee small among the heathen: thou art greatly despised [Obad. 2].**

This great people—they *were* a great people, as we are going to see in this book—are now going to be brought down. Obadiah gives this as a prophecy which looks to the future, but from where we stand today, we see that it has been fulfilled.

What was the great sin of Edom which brought about God's judgment upon her?

> **The pride of thine heart hath deceived thee, thou that dwellest in the clefts of the rock, whose habitation is**

**high; that saith in his heart, Who shall bring me down
to the ground? [Obad. 3].**

"The pride of thine heart hath deceived thee." What was it for which
God hated Edom? It was *pride*. I am confident that the minute I say
this, the wind is taken out of the sails of many of my readers. They are
going to say, "Is that *all*? Pride is bad, but it's not that bad, is it?"

Let me illustrate to you how we today have things all out of propor-
tion concerning sin. Suppose that I knew of a certain Christian who
was drinking very heavily and that I came to ask your advice as to what
his church should do with him. I am sure that you would say that he
ought to be put out of the membership of the church, and I would
agree with you. Now suppose that I told you of an officer in a church
who was caught by the police the other night in a supermarket as he
was breaking into the safe. I'm sure that you would say he ought to be
put out of the church and that he ought to be disciplined. I'd agree
with you on that. Suppose, though, that I told you that I knew of a
certain church member who was filled with pride, who was one of the
proudest persons I had ever met. I dare say that you would not suggest
that he be put out of the church. Many who have a very tender heart
would say, "I think the pastor should talk to him and tell him that it's
wrong to have pride. But it's not such a bad sin after all. At least, it's
one that doesn't show. It's not like getting drunk; it's not like stealing;
it's not like lying." Would I surprise you if I told you that in the sight of
God, pride is a much worse sin than getting drunk? Now the Bible
does have a great deal to say about the sin of drunkenness. God condemns drunkenness. It contributed to the downfall of Israel, Babylon,
the kingdom of Alexander the Great, and Rome. It has brought down
all the great nations, and it will bring down our nation. But, may I say
to you, in God's sight, pride is worse than drunkenness. This is something which gets right down to where we live today. This is right
where the bat hits the ball. This is where the plane of your life and my
life touches down on the runway of the life of God. We are given here a
proper perspective concerning pride. Pride is the sin of sins. It is one
of the worst sins of all. It is something that Scripture condemns above
everything. God has said that He hates pride, and if that is the thing

that Edom is eaten up with, God can say, "Esau have I hated because of his pride."

Notice what the writer of the Proverbs says: "These six things doth the LORD hate: yea, seven are an abomination unto him." And then he gives us the list: (1)"A proud look"; (2)"a lying tongue"; (3)"hands that shed innocent blood"; (4)"an heart that deviseth wicked imaginations"; (5)"feet that be swift in running to mischief"; (6)"a false witness that speaketh lies"; and (7)"and he that soweth discord among brethren" (Prov. 6:16–19). Do you see what is number one on God's hate parade? A proud look. When a man or woman walks into church and looks at some poor saint who is known to have committed a sin, and that man lifts his head and puts his nose in the air, or the woman draws her skirts about her, that, in the sight of God, is worse than getting drunk. This is not to condone drunkenness; it is saying that drunkenness is bad, but pride is much worse.

This is not all that God has to say about pride. God says that He resists the proud, but He is always on the side of the humble. "The fear of the LORD is to hate evil: pride, and arrogancy, and the evil way, and the froward mouth, do I hate" (Prov. 8:13). John tells us, ". . . the pride of life, is not of the Father . . ." (1 John 2:16). Where does the pride of life come from? If there is anything that comes from the Devil, that is it.

A great many saints today have pride of race, pride of face, and pride of grace—they are even proud they have been saved by grace! My friend, your salvation ought not to make you proud; it is not even something to brag about. It is something about which to glorify God, and it is something that should humble you. Aren't you ashamed of yourself that you have to be saved by grace because you are such a miserable sinner? I wish I had something to offer God for salvation, but I have nothing. Therefore, I must be saved by grace, and I cannot even boast of that. There are too many folk boasting of the fact that they have been sinners. God gives grace to the humble. Paul writes, "Let this mind be in you, which was also in Christ Jesus" (Phil. 2:5). What kind of mind did He have? Lowliness of mind. He said, "Take my yoke upon you, and learn of me; for I am meek and lowly in heart . . ." (Matt. 11:29). Pride is that which is destroying the testimony of many Christians and has made them very ineffective for God. They go in for show, but the thing they are building is a big haystack. They are not building on the foundation of Christ with gold and silver and precious stones. Pride has a great many saints down for the count of ten; it has pinned the shoulders of many to the mat today.

Pride, after all, was the sin of Satan. He said, "I will exalt my throne above the stars of God . . . .I will be like the most High" (see Isa. 14:13-14). Pride was also actually the root of Nebuchadnezzar's insanity. He strutted like a peacock in the palace of his kingdom of Babylon. "The king spake, and said, Is not this great Babylon, that I have built for the house of the kingdom by the might of my power, and for the honour of my majesty?" (Dan. 4:30). And what happened to Nebuchadnezzar? "While the word was in the king's mouth, there fell a voice from heaven saying, O king Nebuchadnezzar, to thee it is spoken; The kingdom is departed from thee. And they shall drive thee from men, and thy dwelling shall be with the beasts of the field . . ." (Dan. 4:31-32). That was no accident, my friend. The psychologists today would call Nebuchadnezzar's condition hysteria which leads to a form of amnesia. This man did not know who he was, and he went out and acted like an animal of the field. Why? Because, when a man is lifted up with pride, he's not lifted up but has come *down* to the level of beasts. God debased Nebuchadnezzar and brought him down to the level of the beasts of the field.

What is pride? Let me give you a definition of it: Pride of heart is the attitude of a life that declares its ability to live without God. We find here in the Book of Obadiah that pride of heart had lifted up this nation of Edom just like Esau who had despised his birthright. Even in the home of Isaac, where there was plenty to eat, he liked that bowl of soup, and he liked it more than he liked his birthright. He didn't care for God at all. In despising that birthright, he despised God. And now Esau had become a great nation that had declared its ability to live without God.

"Thou that dwellest in the clefts of the rock, whose habitation is high; that saith in his heart, Who shall bring me down to the ground?" He lived in a very unique place. He lived in the rocky mountain fastness of the rock-hewn city of Petra. It is still in existence today and can be viewed. Many who see it are overwhelmed by the size of the city. It is a ready-made city hewn out of the rock. It is protected by the entrance way which is very narrow in places. A horse and rider can get through but with just a bit of twisting and turning. It was, therefore, a city which could easily be defended. Everything was secure. It was like the First National Bank in that many of the nations of the world deposited vast sums of gold and silver there because they felt that the city could never be taken.

They dwelt "in the clefts of the rock." They were living in great buildings which were hewn out of solid rock inside this great canyon and up and down the sides of it. They were perfectly secure—at least they thought they were. The Edomites had signed a declaration of independence. They had a false sense of security and had severed all relationship with God. They had seceded from the government of God. They had revolted and rebelled against Him.

Now what is God going to do in a case like this?

> **Though thou exalt thyself as the eagle, and though thou set thy nest among the stars, thence will I bring thee down, saith the LORD [Obad. 4].**

"Though thou exalt thyself as the eagle." The eagle is used in Scripture as a symbol of deity. The Edomites were going to overthrow God as Satan had attempted to do, and they were going to become deity. They were going to handle the business that God was supposed to handle. "And though thou set thy nest among the stars"—this was the sin of Satan, for he sought to exalt his throne above the stars. God says, "Thence will I bring thee down."

How many people today are attempting to run their lives as if they were God? They feel that they don't need God, and they live without Him. The interesting thing is that when God made us, He did not put a steering wheel on any of us. Why? Because *He* wants to guide our lives. He wants us to come to Him for salvation first, and then He wants to take charge of our lives. When you and I run our lives, we are in the place of God. We are in the driver's seat. We are the ones who are the captains of our own little ships or our own little planes, and we are going through the water or the air just to suit ourselves. That is pride, and anyone who reaches that position, if he continues in it, is committing a sin which is fatal because it means he will go into a lost eternity.

Will you come now and look down into the microscope again? Edom is the incarnation of Esau. There stands Esau. What do you see? You see a human animal; you see animalism in the raw. Oh, the terrifying ugliness of it all! At this point you may say to me, "I thought we descended from animals, but here you are saying that men act like animals." That is exactly what I am saying, my friend. We didn't descend up, we descended down. There has been no ascension, there has been a descension.

The teaching of evolution as a fact of science is the greatest delusion of the twentieth century. When we do come out of the fog, the unbeliever will move to another explanation for the origin of things. Actually, evolution does not give the origin of things at all. It has been accepted by the average man as gospel truth because he has been brainwashed through radio, television, our schools, and our publications to believe that evolution is a proven fact—and it absolutely is not. The strong and intelligent objections that have been given by reliable scientists are entirely ignored today. I am not going to discuss the pros and cons of evolution—that is not my point—but it is something that I became interested in even before I was sixteen years of age. I had a great desire to read and study, and I appealed to the wrong man, a minister who was a liberal, and he urged me to read Darwin. I read *The Origin of Species, The Descent of Man*, and other miscellaneous papers. I studied it, of course, later in college and again in a denominational seminary. At the seminary they taught theistic evolution, which is probably the most absurd of all interpretations of the origin of things. I want to say to you that I totally reject the godless propaganda of evolution—this idea that it is from mud to man, from protoplasm to personality, from amoeba to animation! I would like to dismiss the argument with a quotation from Dr. Edwin Conklin, the biologist, who said: "The probability of life originating from accident is comparable to the probability of the unabridged dictionary resulting from an explosion in a printing shop." That is good enough for me.

The chief difficulty with the theory of evolution is its end results.

Evolution leads to an awful, fatal pessimism. It leads man to believe that he has arrived, that he is something, that he is actually up at the top; and that belief has led to a fatal pessimism today. That pessimism is seen in our colleges and in the alarming rate of suicide among young people. I attribute it to the teaching of evolution. It was Dr. Albert Einstein who made this statement: "The man who regards his own life and that of his fellow creatures as meaningless is not merely unfortunate but almost disqualified for life." That is a good statement.

If you want to see how this teaching has affected men, listen to the poetry of the late Wystan Hugh Auden:

> Were all the stars to disappear or die,
> I should learn to look at an empty sky
> And feel its total dark sublime,
> Though this might take me a little time.

How pessimistic! And then he added this:

> Looking up at the stars, I know quite well
> That, for all they care, I can go to hell.

May I say to you, that is pessimism, and that is the thinking to which evolution has led.

But wait just a minute! The startling and amazing thing is that the little Book of Obadiah is God's trenchant answer to evolution, and this is the reason He said what He did about Edom.

On Wilshire Boulevard in Los Angeles there are what are known as the La Brea Tar Pits, where they have also now built a great museum. The tar pits and this museum are a tourist attraction in Southern California. When I first came to California as a tourist, I went there when it was just a small museum. The museum showed, according to the scientists, how man lived one hundred thousand to two hundred thousand years ago in California. They showed that he lived like an animal and that he looked like an animal, according to the picture that they displayed. By the way, they didn't have a photograph of him. The fellow must have turned around before they could get the picture! Of course, they didn't have a photograph but composed an imaginary picture of him.

God has something to say to us, my friend. Will you hear me carefully? Why go back one hundred thousand years? Right this moment, if you were to ride down that same Wilshire Boulevard, you would see men and women who are living like animals. They don't look like animals—some of them are called "the beautiful people"—but they are living like animals. The fact is that they have come down from the high plane where God had created them to the plane where they do not depend on God. Not only do they live like animals, they live lower than animals. No animal gets drunk or beats his wife or shoots his children or murders or practices homosexuality. Only mankind does that. Man lives in our day lower than animals, and they were living like that yonder in Edom in Obadiah's day.

You may have heard the story of the pig in Kentucky that got out of its pen, wandered out in the woods, and found a still. Mash had leaked out of this still, and the pig began to eat it and also to drink the liquid leaking out with it. The pig got drunk, and I mean drunk. He couldn't walk, and he sprawled right down in the mud. He stayed there for twenty-four hours until he sobered up. Then as he started off grunting, he was heard to say, "I'll never play the man again."

Or, as someone else has expressed it:

How well do I remember,
'Twas in the bleak December
As I was strolling down the street in many pride,
When my heart began to flutter
And I fell into a gutter,
And a pig came up and lay down by my side.

As I lay there in the gutter,
My heart still all a-flutter,
A man passing by did chance to say,
"You can tell a man that boozes

By the company he chooses,"
And the pig got up and slowly walked away.
                                          —Unknown

No, my friend, man has not evolved from the animal world. Tremendous though his achievements are, man can sink lower than an animal when he determines that he is going to live without God.

Remember that God said to the Edomites: "Though thou exalt thyself as the eagle, and though thou set thy nest among the stars, thence will I bring thee down."

Obadiah continues to set forth the complete destruction of Edom—

> **If thieves came to thee, if robbers by night, (how art thou cut off!) would they not have stolen till they had enough? if the grapegatherers came to thee, would they not leave some grapes? [Obad. 5].**

Obadiah is saying that if a thief came to rob them, he would take only what he wanted—he wouldn't take everything. That would also be true of a grape gatherer—he would leave some grapes. But God said to Edom, "When I judge you, the destruction will be complete."

> **How are the things of Esau searched out! how are his hidden things sought up! [Obad. 6].**

This is the key verse to the Book of Obadiah. "How are the things of Esau searched out!" Let me repeat that Ginsburg, the Hebrew scholar, translates this, "How are the things of Esau stripped bare!" Or, as we have put it, God has put Esau under a microscope, and God says, "Come look. Look through the Word of God, and look at this man. I hate him. Why do I hate him? It is because of his pride of life. He has turned his back on Me and has declared his ability to live without Me." That is the pride of life, my friend.

"How are his hidden things sought up!" Frankly, when I read the story of Esau back in the Book of Genesis, I don't quite understand it, but although I missed it in Genesis, I sure don't miss it here. I can now take the microscope and go back and look at Esau and see why he wanted to trade his birthright for a bowl of soup. It was for the very simple reason that the birthright meant he would be the priest in the family and it meant a relationship to God. Frankly, Esau would rather have had a bowl of soup than to have had a relationship with God. When you reach that place, my friend, you have sunk to the level of the pig that got down in the gutter.

All the men of thy confederacy have brought thee even to the border: the men that were at peace with thee have deceived thee, and prevailed against thee; they that eat thy bread have laid a wound under thee: there is none understanding in him [Obad. 7].

Edom was a nation which all the enemies of that day just passed by. They just couldn't be bothered with him because he was safely holed up in the rock-hewn city of Petra. However, Nebuchadnezzar was able to get the city. Just as God used Nebuchadnezzar to destroy Jerusalem, the city of Jacob's sons who had turned from God, He used Nebuchadnezzar also to reach in and take Edom, the nation of Esau's sons.

Shall I not in that day, saith the LORD, even destroy the wise men out of Edom, and understanding out of the mount of Esau? [Obad. 8].

Not only was Edom noted for the fact that they were well protected in their rocky mountain fastness, in the beautiful city of Petra, but they also had developed a wisdom and learning and superstition. Petra was a pagan center where there were many "pillar cults." Expeditions have excavated the great high place on top of the mountains round about Petra where bloody human sacrifices had been offered. Also Edom was famous for its wisdom. Job's friend, Eliphaz was a Temanite (see Job 4:1). People traveled from afar to hear the wisdom of its wise men (see Jer. 49:1). God says that He will destroy the wise men out of Edom and understanding out of the mount of Esau.

And thy mighty men, O Teman, shall be dismayed, to
the end that every one of the mount of Esau may be cut
off by slaughter [Obad. 9].

"Teman" takes its name from a grandson of Esau and is located in the
southern portion of Edom. The Temanites were noted for their courage.

CRIME OF EDOM

In verses 10 through 14, Obadiah is gong to give a list or a catalog of
the reasons that God is going to destroy Edom. The pride of life, we
have said, was their great sin, but it led also to the committing of other
sins. Pride is an attitude, but it is an attitude that you cannot conceal
very long. It is going to break out like a running cancer because it is
such a tremendous driving force in man. Your philosophy of life is
going to gradually work its way down into your fingers, your feet, your
eyes, and all your senses. You are going to express that philosophy in
some way. If you are godless, you are going to lead a godless life. If you
are godly, you are going to lead a godly life—that naturally follows.
Therefore, Obadiah is now going to spell out the terrible sins that
came from Edom's pride of life.

You must remember at this point that Esau and Jacob were brothers,
twin brothers, although not identical but opposites. They did grow up
in the same family and had the same father and mother. There was a
struggle between them from the very beginning. There was a hatred
and a bitterness that was never healed. It was never healed even when
they became two great nations.

We find, however, that God had something to say to His people
about their relationship to Edom. In Psalm 137:7 we read, "Remember, O LORD, the children of Edom in the day of Jerusalem; who said,
Rase it, rase it, even to the foundation thereof." Edom, instead of be-
friending Israel in the dark hour when the Babylonians destroyed that
nation, stood on the sidelines and, in fact, became the cheering section, urging the Babylonians on in their brutalities. But God had said
to Israel at the very beginning, when they came into the land, "Thou
shalt not abhor an Edomite; for he is thy brother: thou shalt not abhor

an Egyptian; because thou wast a stranger in his land" (Deut. 23:7). Israel's tie with the Edomite was greater—he was his brother, a blood brother—and because of that, God said they were not to hate him. However, we will see that Edom manifested a hatred and bitterness toward Israel throughout the entire length of the history of their nation.

There are five specific actions mentioned here which are derived from pride, from their attitude that they could live without God.

The first one is violence—

For thy violence against thy brother Jacob shame shall cover thee, and thou shalt be cut off for ever [Obad. 10].

Two things were to happen to them. (1) "Shame shall cover thee." Finally, Babylon was able to capture the city of Petra and take the inhabitants into captivity. There was a period in which they were a captive people. (2) "Thou shalt be cut off for ever." Edom as a nation would be utterly destroyed. It is interesting that in our day we hear a great deal about Israel but nothing whatever about Edom.

Edom was a nation that attempted to live without God, and they were a violent, warlike people. Violence is not God's method. In my country we have discovered that very little can be settled by war and violence. It does not *finally* settle any matter at all.

The second charge against Edom is that they joined the enemies of Israel—

In the day that thou stoodest on the other side, in the day that the strangers carried away captive his forces, and foreigners entered into his gates, and cast lots upon Jerusalem, even thou wast as one of them [Obad. 11].

Instead of attempting to befriend and help the people of Israel, to whom they were related by blood, they went over to the side of the brutal enemy which had invaded the land.

But thou shouldest not have looked on the day of thy brother in the day that he became a stranger; neither

> shouldest thou have rejoiced over the children of Judah
> in the day of their destruction; neither shouldest thou
> have spoken proudly in the day of distress [Obad. 12].

They rejoiced over the calamity that had come to Judah. That is always an action of pride. When you hear someone rejoicing over the trouble that another individual is having, you may be sure that you are listening to someone who is very proud. Pride is something that God says He *hates*.

Now the fourth heartless action of the Edomites is looting—

> **Thou shouldest not have entered into the gate of my peo-**
> **ple in the day of their calamity; yea, thou shouldest not**
> **have looked on their affliction in the day of their calam-**
> **ity, nor have laid hands on their substance in the day of**
> **their calamity [Obad. 13].**

Not only did they join with the enemy against Israel, but they actually moved in to loot and plunder after the enemy had taken Israel away into captivity.

My friend, pride will lead a man to do some terrible things, and one of them is to steal. Many a man, in order to keep up a front in his business or to keep up with the fellows at the club, will resort to dishonest methods. Also, many a man, in order to win a woman as his wife, will actually resort to dishonest methods. Our contemporary society is honeycombed with dishonesty. What is our problem? Well, the root problem is pride. A proud man, living his life apart from God, will drift into this sort of thing.

The Bible is still the best book on psychology. It will get down to the root of the problem in the human heart. Let's forget all these little psychological courses on how to improve ourselves and, rather, get back to the Word of God. Perhaps you did not realize that in the little Book of Obadiah you would find the root of the thing that is leading our own nation to self-destruction—*pride*, the attitude of life that declares its ability to live without God.

Now here is the fifth action that springs from pride—

Neither shouldest thou have stood in the crossway, to cut off those of his that did escape; neither shouldest thou have delivered up those of his that did remain in the day of distress [Obad. 14].

In my opinion, this is their lowest action—they hit bottom when they did this. In this they revealed their animal philosophy of the survival of the fittest. They betrayed their brothers. You see, when Nebuchadnezzar invaded Jerusalem, the inhabitants scattered and many of them fled to the rugged country of Edom where they could hide. The Edomites, standing at the crossroads, would betray their hiding places. When the Babylonian soldiers were hot on their trail, the Edomites would say, "Yes, we saw a bunch of Israelites come by here. They went that way. You'll find them holed up in that canyon." They betrayed their brothers.

Not long ago a businessman in Los Angeles, California, told me that the business world is "dog-eat-dog." That is what man has come to by living without God. Man wants to make a name for himself. He wants to make money. He wants to be a success. What is in back of it? *Pride.* What is pride? It is an attitude of living life without God. It leads men to betray others. It will cause people to betray fellow workers in order to obtain their jobs. Many men pretend to be friends when, in fact, they are enemies. There are many men in government today who will betray at the drop of a hat. It is sickening when you take a good look at our society today.

Although I hate to say it, there is also pride in the church. I was a pastor for over forty years and served with many wonderful, faithful men upon whom I could depend. But I learned to my sorrow that when I had a member on the staff who was a proud young man, he would bear watching. A proud young man trying to get on in the world is willing to climb the ladder of success by stepping on the fingers of those who are below him. And every now and then I would add a man to my staff who, for personal advancement, would even be willing to put a knife in my back although I had been helpful to him.

The head of the Church of England was speaking to a bishop many years ago when he made this statement which has a double meaning,

"Every bishop has a crook on his staff." Primarily he was referring to the crook on a shepherd's staff which is used to correct the sheep, but he was also saying that every bishop had a crook in his staff of helpers. There would always be at least one who would try to put a knife in the bishop's back.

Do you see now why God hates pride? It leads men to act like animals—in fact, the horrible truth is that when a man attempts to live without God, he is lower than animals. Therefore, the Book of Obadiah is God's devastating answer to the theory of the evolution of the species. What consummate conceit of man, living apart from God, to think that he has evolved from an animal when he is *living* like an animal. He boasts, "I have evolved from the animal world, and look at me today!" In effect, God says, "Do you really know where you have come from? I created you in My own image, and you fell—you fell so low that you are below the animal world." Repeatedly God says that He *hates* pride, and He has never asked me to apologize for Him.

To see the final issue of Edom and Israel, come with me to the time of Christ. I see a man walking by the Sea of Galilee, over the dusty roads of Samaria, and through the narrow streets of Jerusalem. His name is Jesus. He is in the line of Jacob. Also, I see a man on the throne during those years. His name is Herod, and the Scriptures are very careful to identify him—Herod, the Idumaean, the Edomite, in the line of Esau. When a warning came to the Lord Jesus to flee because Herod would kill Him, He said, "Go tell that fox . . . ." Fox? Yes. "Go, and tell that fox, Behold, I cast out demons, and I do cures today and tomorrow, and the third day I shall have finished" (Luke 13:32, *New Scofield Reference Bible*). And when the Lord Jesus was finally brought before him for judgment, He wouldn't even open His mouth before Herod. There they stand, Jesus and Herod, the final issue of Jacob and Esau.

CATASTROPHE TO EDOM

For the day of the LORD is near upon all the heathen: as thou hast done, it shall be done unto thee: thy reward shall return upon thine own head [Obad. 15].

"For the day of the LORD is near." Let me remind you that the phrase, "day of the LORD," is a technical expression which covers a period of time beginning with the Great Tribulation Period. You and I are living in the day of grace or the day of Christ. The emphasis in our day is upon the Holy Spirit who takes the things of Christ and shows them unto us. After the removal of true believers (collectively called the church), the Day of the Lord will begin, and it will begin with the darkness and judgment of the Great Tribulation Period. Following that terrible time, the Sun of Righteousness will arise with healing in His wings, which will be the coming of the Lord Jesus Christ to the earth to establish His kingdom here.

"For the day of the LORD is near upon all the heathen"—that is, all the *nations.* When the Lord Jesus Christ has come to earth to establish His kingdom, there will be a judgment of the nations, described by our Lord Himself in Matthew 25. Now, very frankly, it is not clear whether the ancient nations of the past, which have long since disappeared from view, will be raised for this judgment, or if their judgment will be the final judgment at the Great White Throne (see Rev. 20:11–15). I find that the commentators differ on this, but I'll give you my private viewpoint. When I go out on a limb, you better not go with me because my limb may break off, but it is my opinion that when Obadiah says, "The day of the LORD is near upon all the nations," he means that Edom will again become a nation during the end times. If you doubt that this is possible, look at the nation Israel. For twenty-five hundred years Israel was not a nation, but in 1948 she again became a nation. When Obadiah says that the Day of the Lord is near upon *all* nations, I interpret that as meaning *all* the nations, including the ancient nations which will come back into existence and will be judged.

Some expositors believe that Edom will experience the full wrath of God when the Lord Jesus Himself executes the judgment of God upon Edom and her allies (see Isa. 63:1–6).

You see, a nation is responsible to God. The Word of God makes that clear. For example, in Deuteronomy 21:1–3 we read: "If one be found slain in the land which the LORD thy God giveth thee to possess it, lying in the field, and it be not known who hath slain him: Then thy elders and thy judges shall come forth, and they shall measure unto the cities which are round about him that is slain: And it shall be, that the city which is next unto the slain man, even the elders of that city shall take an heifer, which hath not been wrought with, and which hath not drawn in the yoke." In other words, when a man was found slain out on the highway, they were to measure to determine which city was closest to that slain man, and that city was responsible for taking over the case and attempting to find out who killed that man. I think that is a great principle that God put down.

Christians talk about their citizenship being in heaven; and it's true that the Head of the church is in heaven, but the feet of the church are on earth. Christians have a responsibility as citizens of the nation of which they are members to exert an influence for God as much as they can. I don't mean to say that a Christian should jump into politics, but I do believe that God could use many more genuine, Bible-believing Christians on the political scene. Some folk say that politics has become so dirty that no Christian should get involved in them. Well, I am of the opinion that a real Christian, willing to stand on his two feet and be counted, could be used by God in our governmental processes. Our nation is responsible to God, and we are part of it.

This does not mean that God will judge nations on the basis of whether or not they have accepted or rejected Christ because never yet has any nation accepted Christ wholeheartedly. It is a mistake to speak of any nation as a Christian nation. While it is true that Christians have had a great influence on nations like England and our own country, they never were truly Christian nations, and certainly both are far from God at the present time.

"As thou hast done, it shall be done unto thee: thy reward shall return upon thine own head." Edom was destroyed just as Obadiah had predicted. First it was captured by Babylon some time after Jerusalem was destroyed. That was accomplished by getting spies inside the capital, Petra, the impregnable fortress–city. Later, Maccabees further subjugated Edom, and finally, the Romans destroyed Edom when they destroyed Jerusalem in A.D. 70. At that time Edom as a nation disappeared from the world scene and has not been heard of since.

Whether or not Edom will live again as a nation is debatable and makes no real difference to you and me. If Edom is around during the Millennium, I'll be happy; and if it is not, I'll still be happy because I know that God is working out His own plan.

For as ye have drunk upon my holy mountain, so shall all the heathen drink continually, yea, they shall drink, and they shall swallow down, and they shall be as though they had not been [Obad. 16].

In other words, God says to Edom, "As you have done, it is going to be done to you. You will be rewarded in the same way." This is what we call today poetic justice. *Lex talionis* is the law of retaliation. The Lord Jesus said, "As you judge, so shall you be judged" (see Matt. 7:1). Or, "Whatsoever a man sows, that shall he also reap" (see Gal. 6:7). Edom will suffer in the same ways that she caused others to suffer. I very frankly shudder when I consider that my nation was the first nation to drop an atom bomb and that we have been a warlike nation. I do not think that God lets any nation get by with that. The history of all nations confirms that as they have dealt it out, in a similar way it has come back to them. This is something which has worked itself out throughout the history of the world.

In verses 17 through 21 we come to the second and last major division of the Book of Obadiah. It is only a few verses, and it concerns the nation Israel. For Edom it was *destruction*, but for Israel it is to be *restoration*. The little nation of Israel fits into the program of almighty God. Everything fits into the program of almighty God. For every individual, it does not matter who you are, the interesting thing is that had God not thought of you, you wouldn't be around. You were in the mind of God. The great question is: Are you going to be in step with Him? Are you going to move into eternity with Him or against Him? His plan and program *will* be carried out, and you will do well to be on His side.

CONDITION OF ISRAEL

Although God judged Israel, they were not to be destroyed as a nation—

> But upon mount Zion shall be deliverance, and there
> shall be holiness; and the house of Jacob shall possess
> their possessions [Obad. 17].

"But upon mount Zion shall be deliverance." Salvation is to be offered upon Mount Zion for the world. That is where it is offered to you and me today. The Lord Jesus came and died on Golgotha for you and me. He is coming back to this earth again. Although we are told that at that time His feet shall stand on the Mount of Olives, He will be coming into Jerusalem, and He will, I believe, rule from the top of Mount Zion.

"And there shall be holiness." There is no holiness there today. I have been on Mount Zion half a dozen times, and I have not found any holiness there. They are just as far from God there as they are over in the Arab section of the old city of Jerusalem. There is no holiness there today, but there *shall* be holiness when the Lord Jesus reigns.

"And the house of Jacob shall possess their possessions." I like this expression. They are not possessing their possessions today. They are in the land—that's true. They have a nation—that's true. They've returned to the land, but they have not returned to God, and as a result they do not possess their possessions. There is a great deal of difference between *having* a possession and *possessing* it.

CONFLAGRATION OF THE HOUSE OF ESAU

> And the house of Jacob shall be a fire, and the house of
> Joseph a flame, and the house of Esau for stubble, and
> they shall kindle in them, and devour them; and there
> shall not be any remaining of the house of Esau, for the
> LORD hath spoken it [Obad. 18].

There will be ultimate, final judgment of Esau. I believe that "the house of Esau" is a kingdom that will not enter into the eternal kingdoms of this earth which will become the kingdoms of our Lord and Savior Jesus Christ. What is it that keeps them from being there? Pride of heart—that attitude of a life that declares its ability to live without

God. Friend, if it is your decision to live without God, you are going to live without Him not only now but throughout eternity.

CONSUMMATION OF ALL THINGS

And they of the south shall possess the mount of Esau; and they of the plain the Philistines: and they shall possess the fields of Ephraim, and the fields of Samaria: and Benjamin shall possess Gilead [Obad. 19].

The southern section of Judah will expand to possess "the mount of Esau." Those on the west will include the coastland of the Philistines. "The fields of Ephraim, and . . .Samaria"—that is, the northern kingdom—will be restored to the nation, and Benjamin will include Gilead, which is on the east bank of the Jordan River.

And the captivity of this host of the children of Israel shall possess that of the Canaanites, even unto Zarephath; and the captivity of Jerusalem, which is in Sepharad, shall possess the cities of the south [Obad. 20].

Zarephath is way up north between Tyre and Sidon in Lebanon. "The cities of the south" refers to Negeb, the southern part, actually, the Sinaitic peninsula. Israel will occupy all the land that God promised to them. He had promised to Abraham a land that contains about three hundred thousand square miles. Even at their zenith, they occupied only about thirty thousand square miles.

And saviours shall come up on mount Zion to judge the mount of Esau; and the kingdom shall the the LORD's [Obad.21].

"Saviors" should be translated "deliverers."

"And the kingdom shall be the LORD's." God is moving forward today undeviatingly, unhesitatingly toward the accomplishment of His purpose; that is, of putting His King on Mount Zion. He says that He will turn and turn and overturn the nations until He comes whose right it is to rule (see Ezek. 21:27).

Nothing can deter or detour or defer God in His plan and in His program. No son of Esau, no animal, can stop Him. No proud man walking this earth can cause God to relinquish or retreat one inch. He is moving today to victory. The kingdom is the Lord's!

There is only One who can lift the heads of men and women wailing through life with their heads down like animals (only humans look up as they walk; animals look down). Evolution has not lifted mankind one inch. Look at our world that has been schooled in this godless philosophy. The deadly poison of godless materialism and humanism will bring upon us the judgment of God! God says, "Though you be lifted up, little man, I'll bring you down."

But He also says, through the lips of His Son, or Savior: "And I, if I be lifted up from the earth, will draw all men unto me" (John 12:32). Which way are you going, my friend? Down the way of pride, pessimism, unbelief, and rebellion, down, down, down? You who were made in the likeness of God can be restored. You will have to lay aside your pride and come in helplessness to his Savior. He can lift you.

BIBLIOGRAPHY
(Recommended for Further Study)

Feinberg, Charles L. *The Minor Prophets*. Chicago, Illinois: Moody Press, 1976.

Gaebelein, Arno C. *The Annotated Bible*. 1917. Reprint. Neptune, New Jersey: Loizeaux Brothers, 1971.

Ironside, H. A. *The Minor Prophets*. Neptune, New Jersey: Loizeaux Brothers, n.d.

Jensen, Irving L. *Minor Prophets of Judah*. Chicago, Illinois: Moody Press, 1975. (Obadiah, Joel, Micah, Nahum, Zephaniah, and Habakkuk)

Tatford, Fredrick A. *The Minor Prophets*. Minneapolis, Minnesota: Klock & Klock, n.d.

Unger, Merrill F. *Unger's Commentary of the Old Testament*, Vol 2. Chicago, Illinois: Moody Press, 1982.